How to Serve

Metropolitan Youssef

How to Serve
By Metropolitan Youssef

Designed & Published by:
St. Mary & St. Moses Abbey Press
101 S Vista Dr, Sandia, TX 78383
stmabbeypress.com

Contents

1

What is Service?

1. A Sacrifice

Service is considered a sacrifice. In the epistle to the Hebrews, St. Paul says, "But do not forget to do good and to share, for with such sacrifices God is well pleased."[30] Not only are we to take this verse to be about charitable deeds, but it can also be understood concerning service, like Sunday school service. In charitable deeds, I may help someone with money. I may give someone food or drink. Also, Sunday school service is definitely considered doing good because I provide spiritual food and the water of life. This is considered one of the best services I can do for someone. If I feed their bodies, the body will die one day. But if I feed their spirit, this will take them to eternal life.

Now, about sharing, he said, "Do not forget to do good and to share."[31] I share my time, my knowledge, and

30 Hebrews 13:16.

31 Ibid.

my emotions. So in Sunday school, there is a lot of sharing between servants and their students. St. Paul considered sharing a sacrifice, with which God is well pleased.

Sacrifice means that we give to others because of our love for God. In Sunday school service, we give of our time, our effort, our emotions, and our knowledge. We give because we love God. That is why, when our Lord Jesus Christ went around preaching from one place to another, His ministry was considered service. As the Lord said about Himself, "The Son of Man did not come to be served, but to serve."[32] The Lord Jesus Christ, before offering Himself on the cross as a sacrifice, offered Himself when He wandered from one place to another, preaching and teaching the word of God. The description of both St. John the Baptist and the Lord Jesus Christ, in their ministry, shows that they were traveling and wandering from one place to another, saying, "Repent, for the kingdom of heaven is at hand!"[33]

As Sunday school servants, if you see that one of your students is sick, you will go and ask about them. If you see that one of your students is poor and needy, you will address their need through the church by coordinating with the priests. Therefore, besides teaching Sunday school, our responsibility toward our children, out of the sacrifice of love, is to take care of all their needs, not only the spiritual needs, but also their physical and psychological needs.

32 Matthew 20:28.

33 Matthew 3:2, 4:17.

That is what we call a holistic approach. You look at the person as a whole. That is why in our prayers, not only do we focus on spiritual needs, but we also focus on physical needs. For this reason, we pray for the sick, for the travelers, for the prisoners, for the air of heaven, for the plants, because all of these provide for our physical needs.

And we also care and pray about our psychological needs. For example, in the Litany for the Departed, we address our psychological need to be comforted. In the Litany for the Sick, we call our Lord, "O You, the true physician of our souls and bodies, the Bishop of all flesh." Also, in feast celebrations, the Church brings joy to our hearts, which again addresses our psychological needs. When somebody is in trouble, we pray for them and comfort them, providing for their psychological needs. In the conclusion of the Watos Theotokias of Midnight Praises, we say, "The sick, heal them. Those who slept, O Lord, repose them. And all our brethren in distress, help us, my Lord, and all of them." So we pray for the sick, asking for physical needs. We pray for the departed and those who are in affliction, addressing the psychological needs. Therefore, the first definition of service is sacrifice. In giving a sacrifice of love, we give without limit, because we love God.

2. Using Our Talents for God's Glory

In the parable of the talents, when the master gave one servant five talents, the second two talents, and the third, one talent, and he asked them to trade with them. The Lord told the person who did not trade with his talent but buried it, "You wicked and lazy servant."[34] All of us, without exception, have received talents from God. Therefore, we must use these talents to minister to one another and to serve one another. As St. Peter said, "As each one has received a gift, minister it to one another, as good stewards of the manifold grace of God."[35] I would like to emphasize the words, "as each one," for each one of us has received a gift.

This gift should not be used for my own glory or my own profit. But we must minister it to one another, helping one another with this gift. In this way, we will be good stewards of the manifold grace of God. But if I keep the talent to myself, using it for my own glory, or if I bury it as that lazy and wicked servant, then I am not using my talent in the right way. And God, on the last day, will ask us, "Give an account of your stewardship."[36] So we will need to give an account. God will tell you, "I gave you so many talents."

Some talents are common to everyone, like time and money. All of us have time and money. There are also specific talents given to some people: talent in teaching, for example, talent in leadership, talent in administration, talent in being a helper to others. God will ask you, "I gave you this talent, did you make a profit with it or not?"

34 Matthew 25:26.

35 1 Peter 4:10.

36 Luke 16:2.

In choirs, for example, we can see how the servants used the talents given to them to organize the children, and to teach them and train them to do a wonderful presentation and performance. They are using their talent. When we can do a great deal with our talents, and can have abundant fruits from our talents, this can glorify God. So, am I using my talents or not?

The Apostles were very careful to focus on their talents. God gave the Apostles the responsibility of preaching the word of God. When an administrative problem happened, the Greek widows being neglected in the daily service, it was their responsibility to solve this problem. They could not say, "We are dedicated to the ministry of God," and turn a blind eye to this responsibility. But at the same time, they should not waste their time making sure that the daily service reaches every single person. That is why they delegated and said very clearly, "It is not desirable that we should leave the word of God and serve tables."[37] They were called to preach the word of God. That is why they assigned the seven deacons to this responsibility of caring for the widows and making sure that the daily service reached everyone.

This is an example of how I can focus on my talents and also how I should delegate to others, so that I may not waste my time, because if you waste your time being distracted with so many responsibilities and you do not delegate, then you will not be profitable in your talents.

---

37 Acts 6:2.

If you are distracted, you will not give it the proper time and attention that are necessary.

3. A Responsibility of the Church

When the multitude stayed with the Lord Jesus Christ for three days without eating or drinking, the disciples went to the Lord Jesus Christ and asked Him to dismiss the multitude to the villages surrounding them in order for them to find lodging and something to eat. But the Lord refused this suggestion and told them, "You give them something to eat."[38] Why did the Lord do this? It was very easy for Him to dismiss them, so they may go to the surrounding cities and find lodging and something to eat. But the Lord did not do this.

Instead, He said to the apostles, "You give them something to eat," to teach us that when there is something within our responsibility, we should not neglect it. If they hosted the multitude for three days, then it was their responsibility to provide them with something to eat. That is why the Lord told them, "You give them something to eat." When the Lord spoke about the wise and faithful steward, He said, "Who then is that faithful and wise steward, whom his master will make ruler over his household, to give them their portion of food in due season?"[39]

"In due season" has many meanings. That is, it should be done at the right time. If we give the food

38 Matthew 14:16.

39 Luke 12:42.

later than its time, they might not benefit. Our children are exposed to homosexuality and transgenderism even in the curriculum of elementary school. They are also exposed to evolution and atheism, so we need to give them their food in its due time.

Before they go to school and learn about all these things, we need to prepare them and teach them about the existence of God. We need to teach them about how to glorify God through our genders and about the basic principles of marriage between a male and a female. We should teach them about a life of purity and how to keep our bodies, the temples of God, pure. If you wait until after they go to school, they will learn about all these things and become brainwashed. Then, when they come to church, and we try to teach them about purity, creation, and all these things, there is concern that we are not providing them with their food at the proper time. We provided it too late.

Also, the phrase, "their portion of food," means the food that is suitable for their age and their spiritual growth, and means the amount they need, no less and no more. It is our responsibility to give the food in the right amount, the right quality, and at the right time. Many Sunday school servants nowadays do not pay attention or spend enough time preparing for the lesson. There is concern that we are not giving them the proper food that they need to grow. Nowadays, servants might either read the lesson on Sunday morning before going to church, or sometimes read it at the time of the class. Or they may not read it at all and just speak from their memory, whatever they have retained in their mind. If you do not spend time in preparing and praying that the Holy Spirit may anoint every word when you utter it, then are we giving them the proper quantity of food they need and at the right time?

Sometimes we even go completely unprepared and rely on YouTube videos that are readily available. The point is *not* figuring out how to fill the thirty minutes or one hour of Sunday school. That is not the point. The parents entrusted us with their children, so that we may teach them and build them up in the fear of God and in heavenly wisdom. So it is not just about how one can fill these thirty minutes or one hour. If it were just about filling this time, that would be easy. But rather, it is about giving them their food in its due season. That is why the Lord Jesus said to His disciples, "You give them something to eat."[40] Do we understand this responsibility? We need to provide the food in the amount and the quality that is suitable for this age, and ensure that we provide it in its due season.

4. Human Development

Service is about human development. It is our responsibility to develop the person. Some Sunday school servants encourage dependency, and they are happy that their students are dependent on them. But this is not right. The right thing is to help them develop, becoming

40 Matthew 14:16.

independent, to depend on God, and to reach spiritual maturity. St. Paul discovered that the Hebrews did not grow into spiritual maturity. That is why he addressed this issue in his epistle to the Hebrews, saying to them about Christ:

> of whom we have much to say, and hard to explain, since you have become dull of hearing. For though by this time you ought to be teachers, you need someone to teach you again the first principles of the oracles of God; and you have come to need milk and not solid food.[41]

He was saying that he needed to tell them many things; that is the food. But unfortunately, it was hard to explain because they had become dull of hearing. And then he rebuked them for not growing, saying, "For though by this time you ought to be teachers..." He told them that they had not developed. All these years in Christ, but they still needed to learn the first principles of the oracles of God. It is grievous that after so many years in Christ, some Christians still need milk because they cannot digest solid food. If you do not help your students to grow and develop, they will be like the Hebrews, dull of hearing and still in need of milk and not solid food.

Can you imagine if there is a twelve-year-old boy who still cannot digest regular food? He still needs to be fed with milk. What about Christians who are in Christ for more than twelve years, but still cannot digest solid food?

---

41 Hebrews 5:10–12.

St. Paul told them that he was not happy that they still needed milk, saying to them, "For everyone who partakes only of milk is unskilled in the word of righteousness, for he is a babe. But solid food belongs to those who are of full age, that is, those who by reason of use have their senses exercised to discern both good and evil."[42] "Full age" means those who are spiritually mature. Little children cannot discern between good and evil. They want to play with a knife. And if they have, for example, a loaded gun, they will not know that it is a loaded gun, and when they play with it, they might kill themselves or kill somebody else.

It is our responsibility to help our children grow. Again, it is not about filling this one hour with a curriculum and some activities. You, as a spiritual parent, must look at their development. Are they growing or not? Are they developing or not? Can they digest solid food or not? What about their ability to discern between good and evil? Service should be directed toward human development.

---

42 Hebrews 5:13–14.

2

Principles of a Successful Service

To reach such a level in service, as we said in the previous chapter, there are some principles we should know in order to serve successfully. If these principles disappear, we will never be able to serve in the right way.

1. Christ-Centric vs. Ego-Centric Service

Service should be directed to Christ alone, and we should serve His children in Him. Service is not about serving ourselves, but about serving others. Sometimes we have needs, and we try to fulfill these needs through the service. For example, if I have a need to be loved, I try to make the students become attached to me to fulfill this need. If I have a need to be powerful, because deep inside me I feel inferior, I may want these children to submit to me. Since I am serving my needs for power and control, I am using Sunday school to serve me, not serving Christ and His children. That is why I cannot call such a service a sacrifice. It is rather far from sacrifice. I am not giving, but rather taking through the service.

Also, I may sometimes try to attach the children to myself, not to God. We are stealing God's children. Although I know it is important to have a bond between the servant and the students whom he is serving, if I am compromising the truth in order to please them, so they will be attracted to me, then I am stealing God's children. If you are telling them what they want to hear, not the truth of the Scripture, then you turn into a man-pleaser.

A powerful servant knows how to say, "He must increase, and I must decrease." To say this is not easy. Everyone wants to magnify themselves. Self-denial and taking the last seat are not easy things to do. We see servants competing together, debating who would be the greatest? Who would be the first? Likewise, the disciples had a dispute together about who would be the greatest among them.[43] St. James and St. John wanted to take a shortcut. They went to the Lord directly and said to Him, "Grant us that we may sit, one on Your right hand and the other on Your left, in Your glory."[44] But the Lord told them, "And whoever of you desires to be first shall be slave of all."[45] It takes power to deny yourself. It is very easy to fight to get what you want. Anyone can do it. But not everyone can say with St. John the Baptist, "He must increase, but I must decrease."[46]

43 See Mark 9:34.

44 Mark 10:37.

45 Mark 10:44.

46 John 3:30.

2. Prayer and Scripture

Any service that is away from prayer and Scripture is not a true service. How can you provide the proper food at the proper time without asking for the grace of God and without being educated yourself? In the catechesis that we say to newly ordained Readers, we tell them that they need to study the Scriptures, book by book, chapter by chapter. They need to be filled with the word of God. "Let the word of Christ dwell in you richly,"[47] lest they fill the ears of those who are listening to them with the words they are reading, but they themselves be rejected. That is why, to serve, we need to have a prayer room, in which we spend a good length of time praying for the service, and we need to study and learn the Scriptures, chapter by chapter and verse by verse.

3. Serving with a Vision

Additionally, we need to serve with a vision. You cannot help your class develop and grow without having a vision. I am certain that all parents have a vision for their children, and they use this vision to develop their plan for raising them, choosing a school they will send them to, and the career they feel may be suitable for them. Therefore, having a vision is very important.

The teenagers, who have drifted away from God and who do not want to come to church, who are perhaps doing drugs or saying, "I am an atheist," or "I am

47 Colossians 3:16.

agnostic," or "I am homosexual," these teenagers were students in our Sunday school classes at some point in the past. They were submissive and were learning. If we had been able to give them the proper food at the proper time, they would not have turned to the things they are doing right now. When we have a vision in serving our children, this will help both them and us in human development.

4. Serving with a Spirit of Humility and Love

You need to serve with a spirit of humility and a spirit of love. Do not feel that you are superior to them, making them feel they are inferior to you. But with humility and meekness, you can give of yourself. "The Son of Man did not come to be served, but to serve."[48] Humility and meekness are very helpful, especially in dealing with teenagers who can at times be resistant. When you speak to them with love and humility, most probably, you will win them over. If there is a student who is rebellious and very difficult and does not want to listen, maybe if you treat him with love and humility, you can actually turn this person from a wolf to a lamb in the flock of God.

Some youth, when they become servants, feel they are better than others, saying that they are now Sunday school servants, and the spirit of arrogance starts to attack them. If you feel that you are better than others and if the spirit of arrogance starts to attack you, this means two things: first, you will lose your power; and second,

48 Matthew 20:28.

you do not understand what service is. Service means you wash the feet of others. You are not better than them, but rather God appointed you to wash the feet of others.

Why do those who are arrogant lose their power? Because "God resists the proud, but gives grace to the humble."[49] When you rely on God and humble yourself, God will give you grace. And this grace will help you to be powerful. St. Paul had a thorn in the flesh—an illness—and he prayed to God that He might heal him. In his mind, he thought, if I am healthy, I will serve You better. But God told him, "No, I want you to be weak in your flesh." Why? So you may not rely on the power of your flesh, but may rely on God. God said to him, "My strength is made perfect in weakness."[50]

This is why St. Paul said, "But we have this treasure in earthen vessels."[51] Earthen vessels are very weak and fragile. Why did God give us the treasure of our ministry in earthen vessels? Why is it sometimes that our health or effort is not the best? This is so that the glory of the power will be directed to God, and not to us. When there is any success in the ministry, we know it is not because of us, but because of God. That is why St. Paul said, "God has chosen the weak things of the world to put to shame the things which are mighty."[52] Why did Satan fall from heaven? Because of pride.

---

49 James 4:6.

50 2 Corinthians 12:9.

51 2 Corinthians 4:7.

52 1 Corinthians 1:27.

5. Long-suffering and Patience

Another principle in service is long-suffering and patience. Sometimes we are not patient with our children; we want them to grow and develop quickly. And if they do not, we get upset and mad at them, and we may tell them that there is no hope in them: "You are a hopeless case." I want you to notice your children growing up, because they will grow in unnoticeable ways. From day to day, you may not notice the growth. But if you look at five years ago or ten years ago, you can see the difference. The growth should be gradual. And since it is gradual, I need to be patient and learn how to suffer for a long time, to be long-suffering. When we see our children not growing, this may bring suffering to our hearts. But with love and humility, we can help these children be transformed.

6. Serving with Zeal

To achieve these four things: sacrifice, trading with your talents for God's glory, providing proper food at the proper time, and helping them in proper development, you need to be zealous, serving God with zeal, not with lukewarmness and laziness. Unfortunately, some servants in this generation are totally different from those in the 50s, 60s, and 70s.

For the former generations, service was above everything else—above work, above family, above personal needs. They did not perceive themselves as doctors or teachers or lawyers or accountants, but rather, as servants. Then everything else comes along the way. But primarily, I am a servant. That is why they were very committed, very zealous, and very determined in their service.

But nowadays, service is the last thing by which I define myself. I might define myself by the job I have, or by the education I have completed, or by who my connections are and whom I know. That is how we define ourselves, not as servants. Service comes at the end of the list because we do not give service the first priority in our lives. So how can I call the service sacrifice if I do not prioritize it in my life? Can you imagine if there is a nanny who is very negligent and does not provide milk for the babies at the right time? The parents will certainly dismiss her, because she is very negligent. Now, if I am a lazy servant, how will I provide the proper food in its time? And we do not want God to say that we are no longer suitable for service, like the parents who dismiss this negligent nanny. We must serve God with commitment, with zeal, and thus we can make a sacrifice for the glory of God. Also, when we serve God with commitment, we will be able to provide the proper food at the proper time, and will help our children grow. We will be wise and faithful in carrying our talents.

7. Serving Without Getting Bored

Another important principle in service is to serve without getting bored. As we read in the epistle to the Galatians, "And let us not grow weary while doing good, for in due season we shall reap if we do not lose heart."[53] Do not say, "I asked about this person ten times, and he never answered my text messages or my phone calls. I tried to visit him, but he never responded to me." St. Paul is telling us that we should not grow weary while doing good; there is a time for harvest, a time to reap. Maybe the seed that I planted is still too small. Sometimes we plant certain seeds, and we eat from their fruit after three or four years or more. But those who lose heart, getting impatient and bored, will not reap these fruits.

8. Using the Holistic Approach

I want to emphasize another principle that was briefly mentioned before: the holistic approach. In implementing the holistic approach to service, I cannot focus on one element. We are bodies, souls, and spirits. I cannot focus only on the needs of the body. Neither can I focus only on the needs of the spirit or the soul. But we must serve the person as a whole because these three things influence each other. Our soul influences our body, and our body influences our spirit, and so on. When you hear the phrase "psychosomatic disease," it means a disease affecting the *soma*, that is, the body. This type of disease also causes trouble in the soul, in the psyche. That is why it is called a psycho-somatic disease.

One time, a lady was bleeding for so many years, and when she touched the hem of the Lord Jesus Christ's garment, she was immediately healed. She was

53 Galatians 6:9.

only healed physically, not spiritually or psychologically. When the Lord asked, "Who touched Me?"[54] she was troubled. But the Lord said to her, "Daughter, be of good cheer; your faith has made you well. Go in peace."[55] By addressing her as "daughter," He showed her love and acceptance. According to the Old Testament law, this woman was considered unclean because of her bleeding. But when the Lord addressed her as "daughter," He gave healing to her soul. And before dismissing her, He told her, "Go in peace," which is different from when we say to each other "peace and grace." When the word peace comes from the mouth of the Lord, He grants this person peace. Therefore, any worries or any troubles that may be in the soul vanish, and the peace of God which surpasses all understanding fills her heart and her mind.[56] The Lord healed her physically and psychologically, but what about spiritually? He also told her, "Your faith has made you well." So He granted her salvation, healing for her spirit. That is what we call the holistic approach. When we serve our children, we need to look at all their needs: physical, spiritual, and psychological.

9. Serving with Gratitude

None of us is worthy to be called a servant. Therefore, we need to serve with an attitude of gratefulness and

54 Luke 8:45.

55 Luke 8:48.

56 See Philippians 4:7.

thanksgiving. We are unworthy and undeserving to be His servants. Some consider the service of God as a burden on their heart. How can you consider the service of God as a burden, especially if we know that we are not worthy? That is why St. Peter says, "Be hospitable to one another without grumbling."[57] If you decide to serve others, serve them with generosity and with love, without grumbling, not out of obligation. You need to serve without grumbling, murmuring, or complaining. If we follow these principles in service, then we can sacrifice and offer God a sacrifice of love. We can provide the proper food at the proper time. We will also use our talents for the glory of God, and will be able to support the development of our children psychologically, spiritually, and physically.

10. Being Able to Apologize

Many times, we have difficulty admitting our sins and apologizing, especially if we have become arrogant since taking the title of a servant, feeling that we are better than others. If that is how I feel, I will fall into self-righteousness, and it will be very difficult for me to admit my mistakes. I will always justify and defend myself. Look at St. Augustine, he did not confess to his priest and stop there. He confessed to the whole world in a book called *The Confessions of St. Augustine.* Here, St. Augustine was gracious to say that he was sorry, that he had sinned, and to write it down.

57 1 Peter 4:9.

A strong Sunday school servant, if he hurts somebody or if he does not deal with his class with the proper respect, will be able to say that he is sorry, apologize, and ask for forgiveness without any attempts to justify himself.

3

Faithfulness in Service

In his first epistle to the Corinthians, St. Paul the Apostle said, "Let a man so consider us, as servants of Christ and stewards of the mysteries of God."[58] St. Paul is saying that people should look at us as servants since we are servants and stewards of Christ. We are stewards because we are entrusted with the talent of service; we are not owners. Sometimes in the service, we act as though we were the owners.

There are usually two important characteristics required in a steward: faithfulness and wisdom. The Gospel of the third watch of the Midnight Hour of the Agpeya says, "Who then is that faithful and wise steward?"[59] St. Paul speaks about faithfulness and says, "Moreover it is required in stewards that one be found faithful."[60] Therefore, it is a requirement to be faithful.

58 1 Corinthians 4:1.

59 Luke 12:42.

60 1 Corinthians 4:2.

Faithfulness means to give glory to God. In everything you do, you must do it for the glory of God, not for your own personal glory.

But who can judge whether I am faithful or not? Three groups may judge our faithfulness: Others, I myself, and God. Either I can judge myself and say, "Thank God, I am faithful in my service." Or others can tell me, "You are faithful in your service." Or God can judge my faithfulness. St. Paul, however, says, "But with me it is a very small thing that I should be judged by you or by a human court. In fact, I do not even judge myself."[61] He says that it meant nothing to him whether others judged him as being faithful or not.

People's opinions change from one day to another. On Hosanna Sunday, the people said, "Hosanna! 'Blessed is He who comes in the name of the LORD!' The King of Israel!"[62] On Good Friday, they cried out, "Crucify Him, crucify Him!"[63] Although it is good to get feedback from people, others are not my ultimate judge, nevertheless.

What about myself? Can I judge myself? St. Paul says, "I do not even judge myself."[64] Why? "For I know of nothing against myself, yet I am not justified by this; but He who judges me is the Lord."[65] From St. Paul's

61 1 Corinthians 4:3.

62 John 12:13.

63 John 19:6.

64 1 Corinthians 4:3.

65 1 Corinthians 4:4.

perspective, if I want to judge myself, I will say, "I am good, there is nothing against myself. Yet I am not justified by this." If you stand before God and you tell Him, "I am faithful," will this justify you? No. That is why St. Paul says that He who judges him is the Lord. The judgment of others does not matter, nor even does my own judgment matter. So, if you want to determine whether you are faithful or not, ask yourself this question: Does God consider you faithful or not? Are you faithful in the eyes of God or not? This is very important.

St. Paul continues, saying, "Therefore judge nothing before the time, until the Lord comes, who will both bring to light the hidden things of darkness and reveal the counsels of the hearts. Then each one's praise will come from God."[66] St. Paul says that we should not judge anything before its time, but should ask God to enlighten our hearts. Ask God, who created light from darkness. In Genesis, He said, "Let there be light,"[67] and light was created from darkness. Similarly, God can enlighten your heart.

When God enlightens your heart, He will bring the hidden things of darkness into light. The dark area of your mind, your heart, and your conscience will be brought into the light by God. And God will also reveal the counsels of the heart. God will examine you and search your heart carefully. If there is a wicked way or unfaithfulness in you, it will be revealed. And when you

66 1 Corinthians 4:5.

67 Genesis 1:3.

get rid of all this unfaithfulness and unwise behavior, then each one's praise will come from God.

St. Paul then says, "Now these things, brethren, I have figuratively transferred to myself and Apollos for your sakes, that you may learn in us not to think beyond what is written, that none of you may be puffed up on behalf of one against the other."[68] In the church of Corinth, there were four groups of people: One group followed Paul, another Apollos, the third Peter, and the fourth, like the non-denominational, followed Christ. Then the groups started to boast, saying, "We are the children of Paul." The other group said, "No, we are the children of Apollos." St. Paul then told them not to be puffed up by this because, "Who is Paul and who is Apollos?" They are only servants, only stewards. And we do not know how God judges us, whether God sees us as faithful or not. Unfortunately, nowadays, there are groups in the Church. They say that they are the children of so-and-so. They compete with one another and attack one another, but this is not right. Who is Paul, and who is Apollos? They are just servants of the Lord.

St. Paul then says, "For who makes you differ from another? And what do you have that you did not receive? Now if you did indeed receive it, why do you boast as if you had not received it?"[69] What makes you different from one another? Is it that you are the children of St. Paul or the children of St. Apollos? No, what distinguishes

---

68 1 Corinthians 4:6.

69 1 Corinthians 4:7.

you is your faithfulness and your wisdom, not that you follow this school or that school. Can you tell me which gift you have that you did not receive from God? Any gift you have—leadership, administration, choir, preaching, teaching—any gift is from God. If somebody gave me this gift, why do I boast as if I have acquired it by my own effort? No. I received it from another.

We should know that God is a faithful God. St. Paul in the epistle to the Romans said, "Let God be true but every man a liar."[70] God cannot deny Himself. He will continue to be faithful even if we deny Him, as St. Paul said, "If we are faithless, He remains faithful; He cannot deny Himself."[71] He is a faithful God and loves the faithful servant.

1. Being Obedient

What does it mean to be faithful? The first meaning can be found in the epistle to the Hebrews. To define faithfulness, St. Paul made a comparison between Moses and Jesus, saying:

> Therefore, holy brethren, partakers of the heavenly calling, consider the Apostle and High Priest of our confession, Christ Jesus, who was faithful to Him who appointed Him, as Moses also was faithful in all His house. For this One has been counted worthy of more glory than

70 Romans 3:4.

71 2 Timothy 2:13.

> Moses, inasmuch as He who built the house has more honor than the house. For every house is built by someone, but He who built all things is God. And Moses indeed was faithful in all His house as a servant, for a testimony of those things which would be spoken afterward, but Christ as a Son over His own house, whose house we are if we hold fast the confidence and the rejoicing of the hope firm to the end.[72]

How was the Son faithful to the Father? St. Paul is saying Jesus was faithful to the Father because the Father appointed Him to be our High Priest. He called Jesus an Apostle and High Priest. Apostle is explained in that the Father sent Him to us, to be our High Priest. Any priest must offer something, so let us see the faithfulness of Jesus. St. Paul said, "Therefore, when He came into the world, He said: 'Sacrifice and offering You did not desire, but a body You have prepared for Me.'"[73] The Father did not send the Son to offer animal sacrifices like the priests of the old covenant. But rather, the Father told the Son that He would be a human being; He would have a body, and He would offer this body as a sacrifice. As a high priest, He will offer Himself as a sacrifice.

So, how is the Son faithful to the Father who appointed Him? How did He react? He said, "Behold, I have come—in the volume of the book it is written of

72 Hebrews 3:1–6.

73 Hebrews 10:5.

Me—to do Your will, O God."[74] As St. Cyril said that Jesus is both the high priest and the sacrifice. "He offered Himself" refers to the fact that He would be slain on the cross. It is a difficult task, but Jesus said, "Behold, I have come … to do Your will, O God."

St. Paul reflects on this in the epistle to the Philippians:

> Let this mind be in you which was also in Christ Jesus, who, being in the form of God, did not consider it robbery to be equal with God, but made Himself of no reputation, taking the form of a bondservant, and coming in the likeness of men. And being found in appearance as a man, He humbled Himself and became obedient to the point of death, even the death of the cross.[75]

He is God; He is one with the Father and the Holy Spirit. Therefore, when He said, "I and My Father are one,"[76] He did not take this by robbery. He was obedient to the Father to the point of death. "Therefore God also has highly exalted Him and given Him the name which is above every name."[77]

St. Paul is asking us to look to Jesus Christ, who was faithful to God the Father who appointed Him, "as Moses also was faithful in all His house." In the Old

74 Hebrews 10:7.

75 Philippians 2:5–8.

76 John 10:30.

77 Philippians 2:9.

Testament, Moses was faithful in the house of God, the tabernacle of meeting. Jesus, also, is faithful in the Church that He built on the rock of faith. When He said, "I will build My church,"[78] Jesus was faithful to God the Father, as Moses also was faithful. St. Paul then compared Moses and Jesus, saying that Jesus has more glory than Moses, because Jesus is God who created Moses. The builder of the house has more honor than the house itself. So if we consider Moses as the house and Jesus as the builder, then Jesus has more honor than Moses.

Another reason why Jesus is more honorable than Moses is that Moses was faithful in the tabernacle of meeting as a servant, but Jesus is the Son of God. There is actually a big difference between a son and a servant, and he explained that we are His house. We are the house of God if we firmly hold fast to the confidence and the rejoicing of hope to the end.

How was Moses faithful? When God gave Moses the instructions for building the tabernacle of meeting, Moses was very careful to follow the details of the instructions: the colors, the materials, the dimensions, everything. Everything in the tabernacle of meeting is a symbol and has a meaning. Colors have meanings, measurements have meanings, materials have meanings.

The details of the tabernacle of meeting were mentioned in the Book of Exodus five times: twice in detail, and three times briefly. This shows us that Moses

78 Matthew 16:18.

was very obedient to the word of God. He followed God's instructions and did not say, "No, this measurement is not right. Let me change the measurement. It will look better." He obeyed God completely.

We, as Sunday school servants, if we want to be faithful to such an extent, must be obedient. Sometimes, we conduct ourselves as owners in the stewardship, instead of as stewards. For example, you teach your class your own personal opinion. If you believe there is nothing wrong with dating, social drinking, or dancing, regardless of what the Church says or what the Bible says, then you will teach your children this way. By doing this, you conduct yourself as an owner, not as a steward. As a steward, I will tell them what God says about these things, not my personal opinions. In teaching my personal opinions, am I a faithful servant? No, I am not, because I am teaching my own belief system. Moses did not change the measurements, the colors, or the materials. He was very obedient. He followed the instructions with exactitude.

As Sunday school servants, we need to be very obedient to the word of God, even if we are not convinced and even if we do not agree with it. If this is what God said, then we need to follow the teachings of God as the Church interpreted them for us. Otherwise, I will not be a faithful servant. A faithful servant is an obedient servant, one who obeys the word of God. I am not preaching myself, but the word of God.

2. Being Faithful in What is Least

We see the second example of faithfulness in the Gospel of St. Luke when the Lord spoke about the parable of the unjust steward.[79] This unjust steward was not faithful to his master. After giving us the parable, the Lord said, "He who is faithful in what is least is faithful also in much; and he who is unjust in what is least is unjust also in much."[80] The second principle of faithfulness is to be faithful in what is least.

Let us take, for example, the three young men and Daniel who were taken captives by the Babylonians. The king ordered that they eat from the delicacies of the king. It was entirely up to them. They could have chosen what is lawful according to the law of Israel, and they could have eaten and enjoyed themselves. But Daniel and the three young men decided not to defile themselves with the delicacies of the king. They asked the person who was in charge of feeding them to try them for ten days and see how healthy they would be. And they were faithful in this way.

When the Christmas season comes, many of us who work in companies have Christmas celebrations, which usually fall during the Nativity Fast. And many of us, Sunday school servants, without thinking, break the fast just because it is a celebration, saying, "Just tonight, Saturday night, we will break the fast, but the rest of the week we will comply." By doing this, we are not faithful

---

79 See Luke 16:1–13.

80 Luke 16:10.

in what is least. And if we are not faithful in what is least, we will not be faithful in what is much. And we might justify ourselves and say, "Will God send me to hell because I ate a little bit of meat?" I will answer this question and say that, no, God will not send us to hell. But this is not the point. The point is not whether God will send us to hell for eating a bit of meat or not, but about your character.

Because a person is comfortable skipping two days of the fast, tomorrow he will skip one week, then he will skip fifteen days, and in the end, he will skip the whole fast. This is what we call drifting away. You will drift just for a small distance. Then the small distance will grow bigger until you find yourself far away from the way you want to walk. If we start to compromise here and there, then we are not faithful in what is least, and we will not be faithful in what is much. It is a slippery slope. If you start being unfaithful in something little, it will be something bigger tomorrow, until you lose your faithfulness.

3. Being Faithful in the Unrighteous Mammon

The third parameter is explained in the Gospel of St. Luke: "If you have not been faithful in the unrighteous mammon, who will commit to your trust the true riches?"[81] What is the unrighteous mammon? The unrighteous mammon is everything we own or possess here on earth. The word unrighteous does not necessarily mean acquiring it in a wrong or unrighteous way. The

81 Luke 16:11.

Lord Jesus Christ is making a comparison between the eternal inheritance and everything on earth. Everything on earth is considered unrighteous when we compare it with the eternal glory, the eternal inheritance.

God desires to give us the eternal inheritance; therefore, He is testing us here on earth, to know to what extent we are righteous and faithful in the unrighteous mammon. For example, are you faithful in our tithes or not? That is the unrighteous mammon. If I am not faithful in my tithes, how will God entrust me with the eternal riches? The Lord said, "If you have not been faithful in the unrighteous mammon, who will commit to your trust the true riches?"[82] The true riches are the inheritance of the kingdom of heaven.

Not only should we be faithful in our tithing, but also in our time. Many of us waste time. God gave us time in order to use it for the glory of the kingdom. Are we redeeming the time as St. Paul said in his epistle to the Ephesians?[83] Are we using the time for the glory of God? What about the time for the service? Are we faithful in visitation? Are we faithful in preparing the lesson? Or do we just wake up Sunday morning, search online, and read the lesson before coming to give it? Are we faithful in the time spent praying for those in our classes, name by name? Are we faithful in attending the meetings, like servants' meetings and prayer meetings in the church? These are the basic requirements for the Sunday school service. If

82 Luke 16:11.

83 See Ephesians 5:16.

we are not faithful in the unrighteous mammon, whether it is time or money, how will God trust us with the true riches? We need to ask ourselves: to what extent are we faithful in what God gave us?

Are we faithful in our appearance as Sunday school servants? Do we offend others, or do we glorify God? Sometimes, the way we speak or dress or appear before others can be a stumbling block. As Sunday school servants, people look at you. St. Paul said to St. Timothy that he needs to "be an example to the believers in word, in conduct, in love, in spirit, in faith, in purity."[84] Everything we have here on earth is unrighteous mammon: time, money, clothes—everything. To what extent are we faithful in these things?

4. Being Faithful in What Belongs to Others

The fourth parameter is being faithful in what belongs to others, as we read in the Gospel of St. Luke, "And if you have not been faithful in what is another man's, who will give you what is your own?"[85] We are born naked, and when we die, we will not take anything with us. Therefore, whatever we have here on earth is not ours. It belongs to another. Are we faithful or not? When we come to church, are we faithful in keeping it clean and in good shape? When our children attend a retreat or convention, we should teach them how to behave and be faithful in what belongs to others. Why is it that after any

84 1 Timothy 4:12.

85 Luke 16:12.

convention or retreat, we discover damage in the place? We do not do this in our homes. Why are we not faithful in what belongs to others? Otherwise, who will give us what is our own? Our own means the eternal inheritance.

The Lord Jesus Christ gave us parameters to understand what it means to be faithful according to God's standards. As we said earlier, who will judge my faithfulness? It is not others. It is not I myself. It is God. I can justify myself, but I will not be justified before God. Others can justify me, but I will not be justified before God.

5. Being Faithful Until Death

In the Book of Revelation, it says, "Be faithful until death, and I will give you the crown of life."[86] What does it mean to be faithful until death? First, it can mean "until I die." Faithfulness is a journey. It is not just for a few years in your life, but it is a journey until your last breath.

Second, it can mean that if you are given a choice, either to compromise your faithfulness or to die, which one will you choose? The children of God should choose to die rather than to compromise their faithfulness. That is why the martyrs died. Because they wanted to be faithful to the teachings and the doctrines that they had received, they did not deny God. That is why the three young men were thrown into the furnace of fire. That is why Daniel was thrown into the lion's den. Choose to die for the name of Christ.

86 Revelation 2:10.

When St. Paul was going to Jerusalem, a prophet named Agabus took his girdle and said, "Thus says the Holy Spirit, 'So shall the Jews at Jerusalem bind the man who owns this belt, and deliver him into the hands of the Gentiles.'"[87] The people around St. Paul cried and begged him not to go to Jerusalem. St. Paul responded to them and said, "What do you mean by weeping and breaking my heart? For I am ready not only to be bound, but also to die at Jerusalem for the name of the Lord Jesus."[88] And he thus insisted on going to Jerusalem.

There is a very beautiful story about St. Polycarp, who was a disciple of St. John the beloved, and he was the bishop of Smyrna. The meaning of the name Polycarp can be broken into "poly," which means "multi," and "carp," or "carpos," which comes from the word "crops." So Polycarp means the fruitful, or the one who has a lot of fruit. St. Polycarp was eighty-six years old and was asked to deny Christ at this very old age. His feast is on March 8 (Meshir 29). St. Polycarp replied and said a very powerful word when he was asked to deny Christ. He said to them, "I have served Him for eighty-six years, and He has been faithful to me all these years; how can I deny Him now?" He chose, in his old age, to be killed rather than to compromise his faith or to deny Christ.

Stories such as those of St. Rebecca and her children, and St. Dolagy and her children, and how they encouraged their children to accept martyrdom for the

---

87 Acts 21:11.

88 Acts 21:13.

sake of Christ, show us how people were faithful in their faith. One of the main differences between the saints and us is faithfulness. If we are faithful in the word of God, in the spiritual struggle, in our spiritual canon, in our Sunday school service, in our relationship with God, in our faith, in defending the doctrines and teachings of the Church, then we will be like the saints. As the Lord told us, "Be faithful until death, and I will give you the crown of life."[89]

6. Called to Serve

In the first epistle to the Ephesians, which we read in the first hour of the Agpeya, St. Paul says, "I, therefore, the prisoner of the Lord, beseech you to walk worthy of the calling with which you were called."[90] As a Christian, I need to walk as a Christian. When God called us to be servants or when God called us to be clergy, He expects from us more than what He expects from ordinary people. In our behavior as well as in our conduct, God expects us to be different. In the Old Testament, there was the law of the Nazirite.

If you dedicate yourself to the service of God, then you need to abide by certain rules and regulations. The same is true for the Levites and the priests, not only regulations regarding the service rituals, but also laws that, for example, prohibited the tribe of Levi from inheriting land in the Promised Land. They may have felt

89 Revelation 2:10.

90 Ephesians 4:1.

discriminated against: Every other tribe would inherit a piece of land in the Promised Land, but this tribe was forbidden to inherit anything in the Promised Land. Why? Because their portion is the Lord.

How often, when we serve the Lord, are we looking to have an inheritance in the dust of this world? Yes, they were given houses to live in, but there was no inheritance for them. We read in the epistles of St. Paul to Timothy and to Titus that he said that there are certain requirements for priests, deacons, and bishops. Then we, as Sunday school servants, have more requirements than what is required of any Christian, and we need to abide by these requirements. As St. Paul said, "I beseech you to walk worthy of the calling with which you were called." You are called to be Sunday school servants. You need to walk worthy of this calling.

One year, we sent a letter of commitment to the Sunday school servants to read it, sign it, and abide by the instructions regarding behavior. Some servants agreed and signed it joyfully, but we saw resistance from many servants. If, as a Sunday school servant, you feel that you cannot abide by these requirements, which are only basic Christian requirements to conduct yourself by, then are you walking worthy of the calling with which you were called, or not? Thus, faithfulness is found in the eyes of God, not in the eyes of others, and not in your own eyes.

As we are examining ourselves, we need to ask ourselves: Are we faithful servants or not? St. Paul says,

"It is required in stewards that one be found faithful."[91] I pray that we can examine ourselves in this area and make a commitment before God to help us be faithful in serving Him with righteousness and faithfulness all the days of our lives.

---

91 1 Corinthians 4:2.

4

False Contentment in Service

Many times when we review or examine our service, we feel content, and we feel there is nothing more we can do. Thank God everything is ok: I have prepared my lesson, I have asked about my children, I have done this and that, and there is nothing more I can do.

This contentment can be a real challenge to progress and advancement in the service. I think what will help the person develop their service and grow more is to think about what could have been done and yet was not done. When we think this way, we will develop ourselves. But as long as we say that there is nothing more to be done than what we are doing, and we feel content, this can kill any development in the service. That is why I would like to discuss six points that can kill any progress or advancement in your service.

1. Lack of Creativity

The first point is a lack of creativity and serving in the same way that you learned and used to serve ten, fifteen, or forty years ago. In our minds, service has a certain shape, a certain way it must be done, and we do not think outside the box. Fifty or sixty years ago, they used to just gather the class, and the Sunday school servant would give a lesson, and that was it. We still use this same way of service sometimes, which began sixty years ago, without considering the needs of the students or the challenges they are facing. And many times, we might say that this is the way we were served, so why should we change it?

The idea here is not simply to change for the sake of change, but to think about the needs of the students, the challenges they are facing, the circumstances they are living in, and how we might modify the service to fulfill their needs. For example, our youth are now using computers, the internet, technology, applications on their phones, and social media. How can we teach our children in a way that is actually effective and can influence their needs? There is nothing wrong with following the same teaching style or school of thought that you learned, but you need flexibility and creativity to reach every one of your children.

2. Leniency with "Small" Sins

We are frequently lenient with "small" sins, either my own or others'. These small sins can gradually make me drift away from a deep relationship with God, and my love will grow colder over time. How can I serve without having this strong relationship and this deep love toward God? Yes, the Church is a place for healing. But God is not lenient with sin. Otherwise, why did He pay the price on the cross? Why did He die on the cross? To set us free from sin. We, indeed, accept the sinners. We are all sinners, and I need the Church as a hospital. We accept them to show them the love of Christ, and when they see the love of Christ, they repent.

On many occasions, we avoid rebuking people, or sometimes servants, lest they become angry, or get upset, or leave the Church. That is why we let things go. For example, we accept servants who dress inappropriately in the church, or who celebrate their weddings or graduations in a non-Christian manner. And we say, "Just let it go; we want to live in peace. It will be a big problem if we confront the servants or the youth." But what is the outcome of this? The blessing will be gone from the church completely, and we will not be showered with blessings from heaven in our service.

One person in Israel disobeyed and took from the plunder that they took in Jericho. His name was Achan, the son of Carmi. And when they came to battle against a small city called Ai, they lost the battle. And Joshua, the son of Nun, was surprised. How did we lose the battle? We won against Jericho, this huge city, so how did we lose the battle in front of this small city Ai? The Lord said to Joshua that this was because there was something wrong; there was a sin among you. You need to cleanse yourselves first and to purify what is wrong in order to be able to win.

When we sometimes allow things to go wrong in the church without confronting them, then there is no blessing. And we will be defeated one time after another. Yes, we need to confront gently, and we need to confront it with tears, as St. Paul said, but it must be confronted. We cannot just let it go. We cannot accept servants who are dancing and drinking, and just let it go, lest they get upset. This will kill the service.

3. Seeing No Fruit

What do we do when we do not see fruits in our service? We all know the story of the fig tree that was cursed by the Lord. This fig tree was full of leaves, but there was no fruit on it. Sometimes our service is like the fig tree. We do many activities, many trips, and many retreats, but when we look for fruit, there is none. And the people around the tree are hungry because there is no fruit. They are hungry for virtues. They are hungry to see the fruit of the Spirit in us.

First, I have to examine myself personally: Do I have fruits that befit repentance, as St. John the Baptist said, "Bear fruits worthy of repentance"[92]? I remember Fr. Luka Sidarous as an example of a repentant servant; the priest is a repentant person leading the repentant. The same goes for Sunday school servants; we are repentant

92 Matthew 3:8.

people. Do we have the fruits of repentance or not? When Zacchaeus repented, he immediately presented fruits. Or are we content with ourselves and our spiritual life?

The fig tree symbolizes the nation of Israel, which had many activities: a temple, sacrifices, worship, but there was no fruit. Why? Because they allowed sin to enter. But what did the Lord do? He went into the temple and purified it. He asked those who were selling and buying to leave the temple. The priests and the high priests were very content. They saw what was happening in the temple and were not bothered by it. Many times, as Sunday school servants, we see things wrong inside the church or inside our classes, and they do not bother us.

Not only does it not bother people, but sometimes they are happy because there may be personal gain behind it. The merchants in the temple made deals and profited from the sacrifices they were selling and buying. Sometimes, my service and the wrongs in my service serve me personally in one way or another. There may not necessarily be financial gain, but there are many other gains. I may also get praise, friendships, relationships, connections, and so on. And because of these gains, I let things go. I am content when there is no fruit.

If I am a people-pleaser, I tell everyone what they want to hear, so I gain the love of people. But in the end, there is no fruit. It does not bother me, because in the end, I am benefiting from this gain. Everyone is saying so-and-so is very good, very kind, and so on. But if the Lord Jesus Christ comes and becomes a Servant with me in the same class, what would He do with the class? Would He see the class not lacking anything, or would He kick those who are selling and buying out? Will He make drastic changes in the class? When we serve faithfully, wisely, and honestly, then our classes and students will be heavenly beings, living here on earth with us, and our light will shine before men. "Let your light so shine before men, that they may see your good works and glorify your Father in heaven."[93]

4. Our Personal Spiritual Growth

In the spiritual life, there is no status quo. I am either growing or declining. If you are not growing, then you are going down. There is nothing called, you are steady here. Examine yourself to see whether you are growing spiritually or not. When was the last time you prayed fervently from your heart? When was the last time you opened the Scripture, your Bible, and read from it for your own personal edification while enjoying reading the Scripture? When was the last time you attended Liturgy and focused during the Liturgy on your Groom, our Lord Jesus Christ, without being distracted by everything around you? When was the last time you shed tears before God while praying?

In one sermon, St. Peter was able to move the hearts of 3,000 persons because it was anointed by the Holy Spirit. Why do we say many sermons and many lessons, and yet we do not see this change? Mainly because we

93 Matthew 5:16.

have lost our spiritual growth. What we teach and preach is just information and knowledge. We either read it or heard it, but it did not come from an experienced heart. To have a relationship with God and to grow spiritually mean there is a true fellowship with the Holy Spirit, and you yourself are changing from glory to glory, to the image of Christ, through which people can see Christ in us. To what extent can people see Christ in me? We need to be growing spiritually, otherwise we will lose our effectiveness in the service.

5. Turning into a Routine

We forget that our service is a calling from God, but it has turned into a routine. Most of us do not spend time preparing for lessons. We just read the lesson that is prepared for us in the Sunday school curriculum. This was very clear when the new curriculum was still in progress. Only the curriculum for the elementary grades was finished, but those for the middle school and high school grades were just outlines. Many people asked about when the curricula for middle school and high school would be finished. Why were they asking? Because they do not want to spend time preparing the lessons. They want everything to be prepared, so they may just read it, go to the class, and say the content they read.

We are not waiting for a new revelation from God in order to give our students a fresh and new spiritual meal. We either go back to our old lessons or recite something we read from an already prepared lesson, giving it to our children, and that is it. Where is the work of the Holy Spirit in you personally? Do you not believe that the Holy Spirit can produce within you new revelations, new teachings, spiritual lessons from your spiritual experience that fit the needs of your own class?

Many of us are content, saying that we did our duty. For example, instead of a personal connection with the children or students, I may send one group message to everyone and consider that I did visitation. Yes, one group text will be a helpful reminder. But do not call this visitation. Visitation means one on one; you go and meet with the person, pray with them, read the Scripture with them, and make them taste and see how sweet the Lord is.

Also, many times we do not even prepare or copy what is written for us in the Sunday school curriculum, and instead, we look for anything on YouTube and just let the children watch it. That is why our Sunday school classes became very dead; there is no life in them. Is this the work of the Holy Spirit? No, definitely not.

6. Seeing the Whole Picture

You only serve your class, but you do not see the whole picture. In the Great Commission, the Lord said, "Go into all the world and preach the gospel to every creature."[94] As faithful Sunday school servants, we should make each member of our class a light to the world and

94 Mark 16:15.

salt of the earth. And then, these people will go outside to their schools and homes, and transform the lives of many, bringing more fruit to the Church of God.

But we are usually only thinking about the ten or fifteen people in our classes, and we do not look outside this group. We do not see how our children should be effective in reflecting the light of Christ to the whole world. And that is why there is no growth, meaning that no people are added to the Church from outside. We read that on the Day of Pentecost, three thousand people joined the Church. In a very short time, three thousand people became five thousand, almost doubling. And we read in the Book of Acts that "the Lord added to the church daily those who were being saved."[95]

Now, after 2,000 years, with the knowledge, methods of preaching, and technology they did not have, the Church is not as powerful in transforming the lives of the people because we lost the whole picture. The focus is only on my class, and I forget my duty as a servant and the great commission, to preach the gospel to the whole world.

Let us examine our service, especially in light of the Resurrection of Christ. Christ rose from the dead to give us a new life and to give us an abundant life. Examine yourself and pray, asking God that we do not remain complacent. I am not referring to the virtue of contentment, but rather contentment in our service and spiritual life. We should ask God to give us His Holy

95 Acts 2:47.

Spirit, that we should grow every day in the love and knowledge of God, and should not be content simply with our duties or the expectations of the Sunday school coordinator or priest, but we should look at the whole picture, which is to present every soul perfect in the Lord Jesus Christ, not only from within the Church but also from outside the Church.

5

How to be Successful in Service

Some servants are very successful; others are not as much. What is the secret behind the success of the Sunday school servants, or servants in general? Is it knowledge? Is it talent? Experience? Training? Personality? Spirituality? When you are successful, you will gain the trust of the priest, Sunday school coordinators, other servants, and the people in general. So people can refer to you and say, "Go, talk to so-and-so." Why? Because he is successful.

The Sunday school servant also has an impact on the students in his class, which extends to his family and other people in the church. Our spiritual life definitely influences our service and ministry. But some weaknesses can challenge our ministry and need to be avoided. This is what we are going to address in this chapter: how to be a successful Sunday school servant.

The ministry of any servant should be Christ-centered, as we have said. Christ should be the example, and I should follow in His footsteps. I must ask myself, "What would the Lord Jesus Christ do if He were in my situation?" Also, any decision or choice I make should be focused on the Lord Jesus Christ. Not only that, but the purpose of the service is to see Christ portrayed in every person. As St. Paul said, "My little children, for whom I labor in birth again until Christ is formed in you."[96]

1. Knowledge of the Word of God

By saying the knowledge of the word of God, we are not speaking about intellectual knowledge, or studying the Bible and understanding it so that we can give a lecture. Of course, this is good, but if the Bible does not become a way of life, this knowledge will not help you or the people whom you are serving. This knowledge should turn into life, as the Lord Jesus Christ said, "The words that I speak to you are spirit, and they are life."[97] In the second epistle to St. Timothy, St. Paul says, "All Scripture is given by inspiration of God, and is profitable for doctrine, for reproof, for correction, for instruction in righteousness."[98]

First, the word of God is profitable for doctrine, meaning for you to learn the word of God, and to teach yourself before teaching others. Next, "for reproof and correction" should be applied to myself first before I use the word of God to reprove and correct others. "For

96 Galatians 4:19.

97 John 6:63.

98 2 Timothy 3:16.

instruction in righteousness" means that if I want to know how to be righteous, the only instructor is the Bible. St. Paul continues, saying, "The man of God may be complete, thoroughly equipped for every good work."[99] When you are complete and thoroughly equipped for every good work, then you will be successful.

Without knowing and applying the word of God, you will not be successful. In his second epistle, St. Peter says, "As His divine power has given to us all things that pertain to life and godliness, through the knowledge of Him who called us by glory and virtue."[100] Anything we need in order to live a godly life is given to us. How does God give us everything pertaining to life and godliness? St. Peter says, "Through the knowledge of Him." How can we know Him? In the Bible, in the word of God, because the word of God is given by inspiration of the Holy Spirit.[101]

You cannot be a successful servant unless you read the word of God, understand it, and apply it in your life. The description St. Paul gave in his epistle to the Ephesians is very fitting for those who do not read the word of God. He said, "Having their understanding darkened, being alienated from the life of God, because of the ignorance that is in them, because of the blindness of their heart."[102] If I do not read the word of God, this is darkness, and I will be alienated from life with God. Alienation from life with God leads to ignorance, blindness, and darkness.

99 2 Timothy 3:17.

100 2 Peter 1:3.

101 See 2 Timothy 3:16.

102 Ephesians 4:18.

When you ask some people why they do not read the Bible, the most common answer is that they do not understand it. But now many commentaries on the Bible are readily available. One of my favorite verses is from the Book of Proverbs, which says, "How long, you simple ones, will you love simplicity? For scorners delight in their scorning, and fools hate knowledge."[103] The word "simplicity" in Arabic is translated to "ignorance." How long, you ignorant ones, will you love ignorance? If you say, "I do not understand the Bible," and that is it, then you love ignorance. Go, read and study. Many commentaries are available. Fools hate knowledge.

Therefore, the first step for success is to have your mind enlightened, not only through knowledge but also through applying the knowledge. Applying the knowledge means to walk in the fear of God. In the Book of Proverbs, it says, "The fear of the Lord is the beginning of wisdom,"[104] and, "He who wins souls is wise."[105] Therefore, you need wisdom to win souls. How can we be wise? "The fear of the Lord is the beginning of wisdom, and the knowledge of the Holy One is understanding."[106] I cannot emphasize enough the importance of studying, memorizing, and living by the word of God. It will enlighten your mind and will make you walk in the fear of God. It will make you wise. David the prophet says:

---

103 Proverbs 1:22.

104 Proverbs 9:10.

105 Proverbs 11:30.

106 Proverbs 9:10.

> You, through Your commandments, make me wiser than my enemies; for they are ever with me. I have more understanding than all my teachers, for Your testimonies are my meditation. I understand more than the ancients, because I keep Your precepts.[107]

Oftentimes, Satan will attack us. How can we respond to his attacks? How did the Lord respond to the three temptations of the devil on the mount? He said, "It is written…" Therefore, the word of God will help us defeat the attacks of the devil. As St. Paul said, "Casting down arguments and every high thing that exalts itself against the knowledge of God, bringing every thought into captivity to the obedience of Christ."[108] When Satan starts to argue with me or tries to convince me of falsehoods, sowing doubts in my heart to make me believe a lie, I can cast down these arguments through the word of God.

There is an especially scary verse that was repeated twice in the Book of Proverbs, which says, "There is a way that seems right to a man, but its end is the way of death."[109] How can I have discernment? Although something seems right, it deceives me. What would protect me from this deception? The knowledge of God. Even if the way seems right, through my knowledge of the Scriptures and applying them in my life, I will be

107 Psalms 119:98–100.

108 2 Corinthians 10:5.

109 Proverbs 16:25.

enlightened. Through the Holy Spirit, I can say that this way seems right but is false; its end is death.

2. Focusing on Eternity

Our ministry should be focused on eternity and eternal life. When the Lord Jesus Christ started His ministry, He said, "Repent, for the kingdom of heaven is at hand."[110] This was also the goal of the ministry of St. John the Baptist: "Repent, for the kingdom of heaven is at hand!"[111]

This goal is not always clear in our minds. A Sunday school servant may do many activities: sports, music, trips, missions—many activities. All these activities are wonderful, but if the goal is only the activity, then you have lost. You need to think beyond the activity. Will this activity lead people to eternal life?

I remember when I was a Sunday school servant for elementary school, I had an idea to make a children's magazine. So I thought it through and had a complete vision for this magazine. I went to my Sunday school coordinator and told him that I wanted to make a magazine for children. He asked me for the reason why. Unfortunately, I did not think about why. I thought about just doing an activity. I told him that having a magazine would be beneficial. Then he started to direct me, saying that if I did not have a goal, then even the

---

110 Matthew 4:17.

111 Matthew 3:2.

topics written in the magazine would be just any topics. But if I had a goal, then the topics that I chose would serve a purpose, to achieve a goal.

That is why in your service, you need to have a very clear goal: eternal life. "I have come that they may have life, and that they may have it more abundantly."[112] Which life? The Lord told us, "In the world you will have tribulation."[113] But this abundant life is the eternal life. When the Lord spoke about the abundant life, He was speaking about eternal life.

3. Being Spiritual

To reach this goal of eternal life, you need to lead your children to be spiritual people. St. Paul classified people into three types. The first type, he called carnal; the second, he called natural; and the third type, he called spiritual.

What is the difference between carnal, natural, and spiritual? A carnal person is led by the desires of the flesh. They do whatever pleases them, even if it is going to destroy their life: drugs, smoking, sexual immorality, love of money, and so on. If you are falling into one of these sins, then you are led by the desires of the flesh. For example, why does a person choose not to fast on Wednesdays and Fridays? There is no valid reason, except if one is seriously ill; that is the only exception. Other

112 John 10:10.

113 John 16:33.

than this, it is the carnal desires within us. I cannot abstain and stay away from certain foods because of the pleasures of the flesh. That is carnal living. If you are a Sunday school servant and you are not fasting on Wednesdays and Fridays, then you are carnal. How can you be a carnal person and lead your children to be spiritual people? You cannot. And the solution is not to quit the service; the solution is to be a spiritual person.

The second type is the natural man, who is led by his mind. Whatever he can comprehend with his mind, he believes, and whatever he cannot comprehend with his mind, he denies. That is why some denominations deny the change of the bread and wine to the Body and Blood, because they cannot accept it with their minds. Some denominations do not accept the Trinity because it contradicts their mind. Some religions do not accept the incarnation for the same reason.

St. Paul spoke about natural people, saying, "But the natural man does not receive the things of the Spirit of God, for they are foolishness to him; nor can he know them, because they are spiritually discerned."[114] For natural people, the highest authority for them is their mind. And I want to clarify here that there is a difference between something that contradicts the mind and something that surpasses our mind or our comprehension. When we speak about the Trinity, it does not contradict our mind, but it surpasses our comprehension. We describe God as incomprehensible.

---

114 1 Corinthians 2:14.

The third type of man is the spiritual one, who is led by the Spirit of God. This person is the only one who can understand things of the Spirit of God. St. Paul said, "But he who is spiritual judges all things, yet he himself is rightly judged by no one."[115] That is why St. Paul states several times in his letter to the Corinthians that his goal is to make them spiritual beings.

How can you know which one you are: carnal, natural, or spiritual? St. Paul answered this question very clearly in his epistle to the Galatians:

> Now the works of the flesh are evident, which are: adultery, fornication, uncleanness, lewdness, idolatry, sorcery, hatred, contentions, jealousies, outbursts of wrath, selfish ambitions, dissensions, heresies, envy, murders, drunkenness, revelries, and the like; of which I tell you beforehand, just as I also told you in time past, that those who practice such things will not inherit the kingdom of God.[116]

If you are under the control of one of these sins, then you are carnal, especially if you are not fighting it. All of us can be tempted by these sins, but as children of God, we need to fight the good fight all the time. That is why St. Paul said that those practicing such things will not inherit eternal life, meaning practicing them without repentance. That is why the goal is to inherit the

115 1 Corinthians 2:15.

116 Galatians 5:19–21.

kingdom of God. In order to reach this goal, you need to be spiritual and teach your students to be spiritual.

Then St. Paul said that spiritual people will bear the fruit of the Spirit: "But the fruit of the Spirit is love, joy, peace, longsuffering, kindness, goodness, faithfulness, gentleness, self-control."[117] We need to be spiritual. St. Paul says in his epistle to the Romans, "Therefore do not let sin reign in your mortal body, that you should obey it in its lusts. And do not present your members as instruments of unrighteousness to sin, but present yourselves to God as being alive from the dead, and your members as instruments of righteousness to God."[118] If your members serve sin, you are carnal. But if your members serve the righteousness of God, then you are a spiritual person, and you have risen from the dead with the Lord Jesus Christ.

4. Developing Your Personality, Imitating Christ

In order to be a successful servant, you need to have a personality that helps and serves others. For example, you must be compassionate toward others. When we study the ministry of our Lord Jesus Christ, we can see that compassion is one of the main characteristics of His ministry. For example, we read in the Gospel of St. Matthew that the Lord Jesus Christ saw the multitude as if they were sheep without a shepherd, and He had

117 Galatians 5:22–23.

118 Romans 6:12–13.

compassion on them.[119] Then what did He do? He spent all night in prayer, and in the morning, He called the disciples and chose twelve, and appointing them as apostles, He sent them on the great commission.

Imagine that you are a Sunday school servant, and there is one youth missing from your class. If you do not feel compassion for him, if you are not concerned about him, if you do not feel worried about him, then how can you serve him? If you see someone in need and you do not have compassion toward this person, how will you serve him?

Service should be the external expression of internal compassion. The person moves first with compassion in his heart, then the service will be the external expression of the internal compassion. If you serve but do not have compassion in your heart, then it will be dry and will not communicate your love toward others. It will be like customer service in any company. The customer service people are kind because they want to win the business. But that is not our goal. Our goal is to win a soul to our Lord Jesus Christ.

If you analyze the good Samaritan, why did he help this Jewish man who was half-dead? Because he was able to see his suffering. If I do not have compassion, I will not see the needs of others. I will be like the priest or the Levite who passed by and did not see the struggles of this person. When we read the story of the good Samaritan, he saw the man, and then he had compassion in his

119 See Matthew 9:36.

heart. He was able to see the need, then he developed compassion, and thus extended his hand to help him. The compassion of the good Samaritan was so strong that he helped an enemy, as there was enmity between the Jews and the Samaritans. When the compassion in my heart is so strong, then I cannot resist even the desire to help my enemies. We need to have a compassionate heart.

Also, in your personality, you must be willing to serve, as the Lord Jesus Christ said, "The Son of Man did not come to be served, but to serve."[120] Many a time, service for us means the one hour that we come to Sunday school class and give the lesson. But are we willing to go the second mile? For example, if you hear about a person who is upset with the church, whether it is right or wrong, what would you do? Do you feel compelled from within to ask about him, serve him, and see what is bothering him? Are we faithful and honest in our visitations? How about prayers for our class? Do you pray for them, one by one, and remember them? If they need any kind of help, do you offer yourself, and do you take the initiative to help them?

One of the characteristics of God is that He gives us more than we ask or understand. He gives us even without asking. In order to be a successful servant, we need to imitate God. Do you serve people when they are in need, before they ask? Sometimes we demand the honor of the servant, but we are not willing to wash the

---

120 Matthew 20:28.

feet of others. That is why our Lord Jesus Christ, before sending the disciples, washed their feet and told them, "If I then, your Lord and Teacher, have washed your feet, you also ought to wash one another's feet."[121] He wanted to tell us that service is very important, and you are called to be a servant, not a teacher. That is what we need to do to serve others, not to be served but to serve others.

To what extent did the Lord serve us? He offered Himself as a ransom for many.[122] Likewise, we should be able to sacrifice our time, our money, our health—wisely, of course—for the service of others. So, your personality in general should have compassion, the willingness to serve, kindness, and gentleness. You must have the fruit of the Spirit to be successful in your service.

Many people move from one denomination to another, not because of theology, but because they saw the image of Christ in these people. When they went to this church, they felt welcomed, loved, and served. People gave them the attention and respect they were looking for. That is why they decided to change their denomination. We must portray this image of Christ in our ministry.

5. Using the Gifts of the Holy Spirit Faithfully

We must use the gifts of the Holy Spirit wisely and faithfully. To be a Sunday school servant means that God

121 John 13:14.

122 See Mark 10:45.

entrusted you and equipped you with certain gifts. As St. Paul mentioned in his epistle to the Ephesians, "And He Himself gave some to be apostles, some prophets, some evangelists, and some pastors and teachers, for the equipping of the saints for the work of ministry, for the edifying of the body of Christ,"[123] that is, the Church. The gifts are the equipment or the tools that we use to build the Church of God and build the people spiritually.

St. Peter said that everyone has received a gift: "As each one has received a gift, minister it to one another, as good stewards of the manifold grace of God."[124] So you need to use these gifts faithfully and wisely to serve others. As the Lord said, "Who then is that faithful and wise steward?"[125] Faithfulness and wisdom. The gifts are like tools, not like jewelry. We use jewelry to adorn ourselves, but we use tools to serve others. The gifts are not given to you to impress others or gain praise and popularity. If that is what you are looking for in using the gifts, you are not faithful because you should render all glory to God. If you are stealing the glory of God and using these gifts to impress people for your own glory or to gain praise, then you are not faithful.

In the Gospel of St. Matthew, they said to the Lord, "Lord, Lord, have we not prophesied in Your name, cast out demons in Your name, and done many wonders in Your name?"[126] But the Lord said to them, "I never knew

123 Ephesians 4:11–12.

124 1 Peter 4:10.

125 Luke 12:42.

126 Matthew 7:22.

you; depart from Me, you who practice lawlessness!"[127] This is because they were not faithful. Also, in the parable of the talents, one person took the gift and buried it. He did not use it; he did not serve others with this gift. When the master came, he told him, "You wicked and lazy servant."[128] Sometimes we have gifts, but we do not want to use them because we may not be comfortable. Why should I sacrifice my time and my effort and my energy? Then we are not wise in using our gifts to win people. You need to know what your gifts are and how to use them for the glory of God. The guidance of your spiritual father, as well as your Sunday school coordinator, will be helpful in this regard.

---

127 Matthew 7:23.

128 Matthew 25:26.

6

Burnout in Service

As we approach the end of the Coptic year, and we are beginning a new service, some of us may have reached a point of not wanting to serve anymore in the new Coptic year. I may plan to talk to the priest and excuse myself from the service. I may think my service is not profitable, and I have no fruit. Also, I have no time, so I cannot commit to the service. It is as though a person were hitting a wall and can do nothing more. If any of us are experiencing these feelings, this is what we call "burnout," and it is a very well-known phenomenon, especially among PhD students. They call it "PhD burnout syndrome." When someone starts doing their dissertation, and there is a lot of work and research that need to be done, they feel burned out, saying that they do not want to continue, and would rather quit the whole program instead. Similarly, in service, we can also experience burnout.

What is Burnout?

Burnout is more than just being tired or busy. It is losing heart, getting frustrated, and being on the edge of hopelessness. As St. Paul said, "Therefore we do not lose heart. Even though our outward man is perishing, yet the inward man is being renewed day by day."[129] We should not lose heart in our service even when we get tired, older, and exhausted. But our inner man is being renewed day after day.

In our lifetime, I cannot find a better example than H.H. Pope Shenouda III. When he was almost ninety years old, and his outer man became tired and sick, his commitment to his service, to travel, to ask about his people, to do visitations, remained strong. In his last sermon, even when he was in severe pain, his commitment to meet the people, to offer his service to God, and to preach to the people did not waver. Yes, his outward man was perishing, but his inner man was renewed day by day. And all of us servants should do the same.

What is burnout? It is feeling that I am unable to give anymore. I have nothing to give. I am completely empty, so do not ask me to serve because I cannot give anymore. It is feeling that I am not enjoying the service, but rather I am injured and hurt by the service because there is nothing I can give. I feel that the service has become a liability to me.

129 2 Corinthians 4:16.

This is exactly like a wick when there is no oil in the candle. When there is no oil, it cannot give any light. That is burnout. It is attempting to give what we do not have. How can I speak to people about peace when I do not have peace in my heart? How can I speak to people about prayer and enjoying prayer when I am not enjoying prayer anymore? How can I speak to people about repentance when I am not living the life of repentance? So it is attempting to give what we do not have.

But if we reach this point, this means we should not trust in ourselves, but we should put our trust in God. As St. Paul said in his epistle to the Corinthians, "Blessed be the God and Father of our Lord Jesus Christ, the Father of mercies and God of all comfort, who comforts us in all our tribulation, that we may be able to comfort those who are in any trouble, with the comfort with which we ourselves are comforted by God."[130] We need to put all our trust in God, asking Him to comfort us and be with us, and then when we receive comfort from God, we can speak to people about peace, comfort, and consolation.

Burning out is when I feel that I am not giving out of love but out of obligation. I come on Sunday, not because I love God, but because I am obligated to come. And so is the case with Sunday school, visitations, and attending servants' meetings. This is burning out. And this is an important principle in the service, as St. Peter said, "Shepherd the flock of God which is among you,

130 2 Corinthians 1:3–4.

serving as overseers, not by compulsion but willingly."[131] That is, not because you feel obligated, but willingly. The will here is the will of love. I love to do this, I want to do this, I enjoy doing this. I am not doing it just because I feel obligated to do it. We may experience this sometimes when we go to work or to school, saying that we have to study, or that we have to go to work. But this feeling should not be in the service or in worshipping God. It should not be out of obligation but out of love.

The Causes of Burnout in Service

1. Unreasonable Expectations

The first reason is having unreasonable expectations. The Lord warned us about this. The Lord suffered in His ministry. People called Him Beelzebub and called Him crazy and out of His mind. They wanted to stone Him and to throw Him off a mountain. They called Him a false teacher, a deceiver, a blasphemer. And He ended up crucified. The Lord taught us that if you serve, you should remember that the disciple is not better than his teacher. So you should not expect honor or glory. This is a wrong expectation. St. Paul said about servants, "We have been made as the filth of the world, the offscouring of all things until now."[132] That is how he described himself as a servant.

131 1 Peter 5:2.

132 1 Corinthians 4:13.

But when we have unrealistic or unreasonable expectations, that is when we start to feel burned out. Let us take some examples of unreasonable expectations: to expect to be honored, respected, or appreciated by others. When you have this expectation, you will end up frustrated in the end because you will not find appreciation, honor, or respect. Many people will actually accuse you because you are not doing enough for them. If they did so with the Lord Jesus Christ, you need to expect that it would be done likewise to you.

When God ordered the people to honor His disciples, He told them, "He who receives you receives Me."[133] We should know that while there is an expectation for people to honor the servants and the clergy, there is no obligation for us, as clergy and servants, to be honored. Let me explain the difference. There is a big difference between God commanding the people to honor the clergy and servants, and God commanding the clergy and servants to demand honor. He never ordered us or commanded us to demand honor. Therefore, if we, as clergymen and servants, start demanding honor and respect, we are on the wrong path. But it is a command for the people to honor and respect the servants of God.

This is the same concept of submission in marriage. God never ordered the husband to demand submission. But He ordered wives to submit. So when a husband comes and tells me, "The Lord says, 'Wives submit to your husbands,' but she does not submit to me," I tell him

---

133 Matthew 10:40.

that the Lord never said that the husband should make his wife submit to him. There is no verse like this. That is the difference between a command and a demand. We cannot demand respect and honor, although the people are commanded to do so.

Another unreasonable expectation in the service is to expect that you will be loved or favored by others. And this is a real struggle. How will I continue to love those who do not love me? If you have some students in your class who do not love or appreciate you, you still must love them and show them genuine love, even if they do not show it back to you. St. Paul said, "And I will very gladly spend and be spent for your souls; though the more abundantly I love you, the less I am loved."[134] "Spend" is from what I have, and "be spent" is to sacrifice. I am willing to be sacrificed for you. See how much he loved them. He loved them to the extent that he was willing to give himself as a sacrifice for them. Even if this is the case, that they did not love him, he would continue to love them.

Additionally, if you do not love yourself, you will not be at peace with yourself. When the Lord said, "You shall love your neighbor as yourself,"[135] this implies that you need to love yourself. But to love yourself means to care for your own salvation, not a selfish love.

There is a story in the Paradise of the Desert Fathers, which goes as follows:

134 2 Corinthians 12:15.

135 Matthew 19:19.

> A brother lived in the Cells and in his solitude he was troubled. He went to tell Abba Theodore of Pherme about it. The old man said to him, "Go, be more humble in your aspirations, place yourself under obedience and live with others." Later, he came back to the old man and said, "I do not find any peace with others." The old man said to him, "If you are not at peace either alone or with others, why have you become a monk? Is it not to suffer trials? Tell me how many years you have worn the habit?" He replied, "For eight years." Then the old man said to him, "I have worn the habit seventy years and on no day have I found peace. Do you expect to obtain peace in eight years?" At these words the brother went away strengthened.[136]

Abba Theodore told him that he should go to live in a community with the rest of the monks, to live with others, placing himself under obedience. But he did not find peace in the solitary life, nor while living with the other monks. The old man said to him, "If you are not at peace alone or with others, why have you become a monk? Is it not to suffer trials?" This monk had unreasonable expectations; he expected to live without any trials. In the same way, when we start serving, we need to have reasonable expectations and to remember that a disciple is not better than his master.

---

136 *The Sayings of the Desert Fathers*, Ward B., trans. (Kalamazoo, Michigan: Cistercian Publications, 1975), Theodore of Pherme 2.

2. Inaccurate Assessment

How do you measure or assess your success in service? What are the factors you use to identify if you are successful in the service or not? How do you evaluate yourself? Pope Shenouda had a meditation on when the Lord descended to Hades and went to Paradise; it is not real, but just a meditation by Pope Shenouda. Archangel Michael met the Lord Jesus Christ and asked Him, "Tell me about Your service. You have served now for three years, so tell me how successful Your service was." So the Lord told him, "One of My disciples betrayed Me, the other denied Me, and the rest fled away and did not go with Me to Golgotha. One of them, St. Mark, fled away naked because of fear. And no one went with Me to the Golgotha except some women and one disciple." Archangel Michael told Him, "This means Your service failed. So after your resurrection, I am sure You will choose a new group of servants because all these people cannot serve." So, the Lord told Him, "No, I will work with the same group." Archangel Michael told Him, "How come? After they failed You? No one even went with You." But He told him, "No, but they are faithful to Me. That is why I will work with them, because of their faithfulness. Yes, they fled out of weakness, but they are faithful."

And this teaches us about inaccurate assessment. Many times, we are goal-oriented. Society teaches us to be goal-oriented, emphasizing the need to achieve our goals, even if we need to step on people until we reach our goal. For example, if the goal of a company is to make a certain profit at the end of the year, they may lay off 1,000 employees, without caring about them; they just need to reach their goal. They will step on anyone just to reach their goal.

We are goal-oriented; therefore, we sometimes define success by attendance, number of people, comments about our sermons, or the spiritual growth of our children. And if we do not see immediate results, we think we are failing. If at the end of the year, we do not see real transformation in our students' lives, we feel that we are failing. Although the Lord said to His disciples, "Others have labored, and you have entered into their labors."[137]

We need to know what true success is. It is faithfulness. You can evaluate your success by how faithful you were in your service. God told the steward, "Well done, good and faithful servant; you were faithful over a few things, I will make you ruler over many things."[138] So the accurate measure of success is my faithfulness. Did I do what I needed to do? It has nothing to do with the fruit, attendance, or transformation of the people. This transformation may happen two or three years after my service.

Constantly trying to measure your performance will either lead to pride or despair, depending on what you find. If you find good results, you will fall into pride. But if you do not, you will fall into despair. Good results

137 John 4:38.

138 Matthew 25:21.

are not achieved because of things I did; they are by the grace of God. And bad results may simply mean it is not yet time for the fruit to appear, more time is needed for the seed to bear fruit, but it will bear fruit eventually. That is why St. Paul understood that you cannot evaluate based on results, that is, based on attendance, comments on your sermon, or how much transformation happens in your people. He said, "I planted, Apollos watered, but God gave the increase."[139]

We are the messengers, not the authors of the message. God is the author of the message, and I am just delivering the message to the people. I need to be faithful in carrying the message and delivering it to you, and that is it. What will this message do to you? That is between God and you. I have nothing to do with that. My job is to take this message, without alteration, without dilution, without any adulteration to the message, and give it to you in its most pure form. That is it. That is success in service. We are just messengers and intercessors; we pray for our people. But we are never the saviors or judges.

Some of us, clergy or servants, perceive ourselves as saviors. You may say, "I want to save this person. This person is getting lost; I will go and save him." You cannot. There is only one Savior, the Lord Jesus Christ. All you can do is pray and deliver to him the message that God loves him and that God is willing to save him. Deliver this message faithfully and intercede on his behalf. In the Divine Liturgy of St. Gregory, we say, "Neither an

139 1 Corinthians 3:6.

angel nor an archangel, neither a patriarch nor a prophet, have You entrusted with our salvation." So how can you think or perceive yourself as a savior, saying, "I will go and save this person"? You are not a savior; you are just the messenger.

Also, some of us put ourselves as judges when we see people doing wrong. We may say, "No, this is wrong; that is right. He cannot do this." We are messengers, not judges. Understanding our role will actually help us to avoid getting burned out.

This problem can be seen in two great prophets who inaccurately assessed their success. Samuel was frustrated after the people rejected him and said that they needed a king to rule over them. He felt that, after all these years of faithful service, he had failed because the people now rejected him and did not want him to be their judge, for they asked for a king. God appeared to Samuel and told him, "They have not rejected you, but they have rejected Me, that I should not reign over them."[140] You are faithful, and your service was successful, in spite of this bad result. Despite all these years of faithful service, the people rejected you and demanded a king, but in front of Me, you are a faithful servant. If we evaluate the service of Samuel based on our assessment, we would call him a failure; he failed in his service. But to God, he did not fail. Why? Despite the people rejecting him after his faithful service, God said that he was a faithful judge and prophet because he did his service in faithfulness.

---

140 1 Samuel 8:7.

The same is true for Moses. At one moment, Moses felt that he could not do it anymore. The Scripture says:

> Then Moses spoke to the LORD, saying: "Let the LORD, the God of the spirits of all flesh, set a man over the congregation, who may go out before them and go in before them, who may lead them out and bring them in, that the congregation of the LORD may not be like sheep which have no shepherd."[141]

He no longer wanted to be the leader of Israel. He asked God to choose another leader who may go out and come in before them. He was frustrated because the people were once again rebellious and stiff-necked. He was inaccurately evaluating his service and felt that he was not successful.

Faithfulness means, am I doing *what* I am required to do in the *right way*? Who is the wise and faithful steward? In terms of wisdom, I need to think about how I can address the students in a way that they will understand. This is part of my faithfulness in service. I need to think about how I can deliver the message clearly, directly, and unaltered to touch their hearts. But again, I am the messenger; I am not the author of the message. But am I faithful or not? That is the question. And the second element is wisdom: am I wise in how I approach my students?

---

141 Numbers 27:15–17.

3. Going Through Difficult Times

St. Paul went through this experience. In his second epistle to the Corinthians, he says, "We were burdened beyond measure, above strength, so that we despaired even of life."[142] And I like the saying, "Pain is inevitable, but misery is optional." All of us are exposed to pain, but how we deal with this pain and difficult times is important. Some people choose misery, yet others choose coping. That is why misery is optional, although pain is inevitable.

How do you cope? Will you fall into self-pity and cry over yourself? You will be miserable at the end. See how St. Paul was coping. He said, "We are hard-pressed on every side, yet not crushed; we are perplexed, but not in despair."[143] Do you have enough coping mechanisms to know how to cope during difficult times and how to get support from God, from the intercessions of the saints, from others around you, and how to benefit from this time, under all circumstances?

Let us take a nice story from the Paradise of the Desert Fathers and Mothers as an example:

> Amma Theodora asked Pope Theophilus what is the meaning of the Apostle's expression: "Redeeming the time" [Col 4:5], and he said to her: "The term indicates the profit [to be gained]. For instance: an occasion for being maltreated comes upon you. Purchase the

142 2 Corinthians 1:8.

143 2 Corinthians 4:8.

> time of maltreatment with humility and long-suffering and gain a reward for yourself. Does an occasion of dishonor occur? Purchase the time with forbearance and get rewarded. And every adverse situation produces a reward for us if we are willing."[144]

All these times are lessons for us. When someone comes to me and says, "I am going through a difficult time," I usually tell them that this is a school for you to learn endurance and patience. How will you learn endurance if you never go through a difficult time? How are you going to learn patience if you never go through hardship? How will you learn forgiveness if nobody ever insults or hurts you? This is an opportunity for you to grow. It is your choice. You can learn from the time of trouble and make it a time of profit, not a time of misery and self-pity. This is what St. Paul may have meant by the words "redeeming the time." You need to redeem the time of trouble and hardship by making a profit out of this time.

4. Neglect of Personal Prayers

The fourth reason for burnout is neglecting personal prayers and personal time with God. This occurs when we just do our physical service, but we do not retreat and prioritize our personal time with God. Physical service is attractive to all of us because it is clear. When I lead the

---

144 *Give Me a Word: The Alphabetical Sayings of the Desert Fathers*, Wortley J., trans. (Yonkers, NY: SVS Press, 2014), Theodora 1.

people, give sermons, do visitations, lead a choir, serve in any capacity in the church, it is clear in front of everyone.

But spiritual service, when I go to my inner room and shut myself in this room, and I pray for my class, my students, nobody sees this. It is between God and me. That is why it is easy to perform and see the results of tangible, physical activities, but it is harder to see the benefit of spiritual service because it is between God and me in my inner room. That is why we tend to neglect our personal time with God and our personal prayers.

What is the result of neglecting our personal time with God? Our service will depend on our own strength, not on God. We will not take our daily manna from God, but instead, we will be serving with our own strength. But how can we serve with our own strength if we are truly fellow workers with God, as St. Paul said?[145] You can give a very beautiful sermon, but unless the Holy Spirit touches their hearts, your words will be in vain.

When you read the sermon of St. Peter in the Book of Acts, you find that there was nothing special about this sermon.[146] He quoted some verses from the Old Testament, and that is it. Many sermons are similar to the words of St. Peter. But how was this sermon able to capture the hearts of 3,000 persons? It was not the words, but it was the Holy Spirit who worked through the words. Because St. Peter was a man of prayer, he spent ten days in prayer. That is why when he spoke, he

145 See 1 Corinthians 3:9 and 2 Corinthians 6:1.

146 See Acts 2.

spoke with the power of the Holy Spirit, and the Holy Spirit moved the hearts of the people. If you do not pray before giving your sermon, then you are speaking with human wisdom. You are just a philosopher. But if you pray before giving the sermon, then you are a preacher.

In his epistle to the Ephesians, St. Paul told us that he was not only a preacher, sending and writing epistles, but he was also a man of prayer. He used to pray and get on his knees in prayer for the people. He told them, "Praying always with all prayer and supplication in the Spirit, being watchful to this end with all perseverance and supplication for all the saints."[147] Even the Lord Jesus Christ, we saw Him going to the mountain and spending the night in prayer. You cannot serve without having your personal time with God.

5. Relying on Earthly Wisdom

Another reason for burnout is turning to earthly wisdom and relying on it instead of heavenly wisdom. When you rely more on the human arm instead of relying on God, you are attempting to solve problems with worldly designs, not by the power of the Spirit of God. Many times, when we face a problem, or somebody consults with us about a problem, we try to find a human and earthly solution to this problem without spending time in prayer, asking God to solve this issue. The first step in resolving a conflict between a couple is to lead both of them to repentance. That is the first step, because we can use all the problem-solving

147 Ephesians 6:18.

techniques and help them to have better communication, but without repenting and returning to God, it is only a matter of time until another relapse happens again.

Many times we speak about the grace of God, and how we need to walk in the grace of God, but we are not leaning on the grace of God, on His heavenly wisdom. That is why St. James warned us against using earthly wisdom, saying, "But the wisdom that is from above is first pure, then peaceable, gentle, willing to yield, full of mercy and good fruits, without partiality and without hypocrisy."[148] That is the heavenly wisdom. Earthly wisdom will eventually fail those who rely on it.

6. Feeling Disconnected

Another reason for feeling burned out is when we do not make a connection with our students in our class. We serve them, but there is no personal connection between us. So, you should ask yourself, after all these months of service, do you feel disconnected from those whom you serve? If there is a disconnect between you and them, you cannot serve them. Knowing those whom we serve and being known by them is a fundamental capital in the success of our ministry. The Lord Jesus Christ said, "I know My sheep, and am known by My own."[149]

This mutual knowledge between a servant and their class is very important. We cannot be part of their lives

148 James 3:17.

149 John 10:14.

by only seeing them at church for one hour every week. If you are not part of their life beyond this hour, they will not turn to you. When we were Sunday school students, not servants, when we had any issue, the first person we thought to turn to was our Sunday school servant, not our priest or bishop. It was very difficult to reach the priest. So we used to turn to our Sunday school servants because we felt connected to them. And this connection still remains with them.

In Egypt, the main Liturgy is on Friday because that is the weekend in Egypt. After the Liturgy on Friday, when we go to the lobby of the church, you would often see a servant surrounded by their students, and another servant surrounded by their students. That is how connected we were with each other. Here, I do not see this connection between the servants and the students; we are not part of their lives. But how will they feel comfortable to turn to me for advice if I am not part of their life? You need to go visit them and connect with them if you want your service to be successful.

7. Spreading Oneself Thin

Another reason for burnout is when you spread yourself thin, taking on too much in the service. Everybody who asks you to do something, and you say, "Yes, I will do this; I will do that," and then you feel overwhelmed and cannot do them. You need to respect your limitations and maintain your boundaries. Yes, you should not be lazy and say no to every service. But also, you should not be without boundaries and say yes to all services. This is wrong, and that is wrong.

You cannot do it all without help. Moses, in the beginning of his service, was trying to do everything by himself, and he was burned out. So his father-in-law advised him, and as we read in the Book of Exodus, "So Moses' father-in-law said to him, 'The thing that you do is not good. Both you and these people who are with you will surely wear yourselves out. For this thing is too much for you; you are not able to perform it by yourself.'"[150] That is why he told him to choose others to help him by delegating and asking others to help.

When we take on too much, we end up failing. We need to understand what delegation is, and when we delegate or train somebody, we need to give them room for failure. Some of us just prefer to do things ourselves because when I ask somebody to do it, I will train him, and maybe he will not do it the right way or do it the way I want, so it is better for me to spare all this headache and do it by myself. But spending the time training others and teaching them to carry on the service instead of you is the right approach. While you are doing this, you need to encourage them even if they fail temporarily. Nobody will be successful from the first time.

8. Leaving Oneself in the Hand of Others

When you leave your responsibilities in the hands of others, you are not in control of your time and

150 Exodus 18:17–18.

priorities. Others set your priorities and determine how you will spend the day. So, here, we need to ask ourselves the following question: Who is leading me? Is it the Spirit of God? Or the demands of the people? That is, what the people want. Many times, people tell me, "That's what the people want." But it should not be what the people want, but rather what the Holy Spirit is leading us and guiding us to do. Are you letting others dictate your priorities, schedule, and reactions? If it is others, they will say that you need to do this right now. "Father, you need to come and visit us right now." They may take advantage of your kindness, and they will set your schedule and priorities. They will set your time and what you are going to do. At this time, you will lose your peace. And when we start to be men-pleasers, this will stain our decisions with partiality. We will be biased, and we will not do things that please God but the things that please men.

Amma Theodora said:

> The teacher ought to be a stranger to the lust for power, alien to vainglory, distant from pride, not taken in by flattery, not blinded by gifts, not conquered by his belly, not prey to anger; but long-suffering, gentle, and as humble-minded as possible. He should be approved and patient; caring and a lover of souls.[151]

---

151 *Give Me a Word: The Alphabetical Sayings of the Desert Fathers*, Wortley J., trans. (Yonkers, NY: SVS Press, 2014), Theodora 5.

Some people try to control us by anger. They get angry, and, wanting to keep them calm, we just do what they want to avoid their anger. But this is not the right way. That is why she said that you should not allow people to fool you by flattery nor to blind you by gifts, and so on.

9. Lack of Patience

We want to plant the seed today and tomorrow eat of its fruit, but we do not want to wait. We want an immediate response. When you click here and it does not turn, you get frustrated. Nowadays, everything is approached with a quick do-it-fast attitude. That is why we start to lose patience. We want everything to be quick and immediate. We need to remember that it takes a lifetime to develop the virtues of a faithful servant. So we should not lose heart because we have not yet attained them or because we are not there yet. We should be patient to wait for the Lord.

The Scripture says in the Book of Isaiah, "But those who wait on the Lord shall renew their strength; they shall mount up with wings like eagles, they shall run and not be weary, they shall walk and not faint."[152] We need to allow the service to be a motivation for us to grow and learn to be patient, not viewing it as a frustration. Do not expect quick results, but rather learn how to be patient. In the epistle to the Galatians, St. Paul says, "And let us not grow weary while doing good, for in due season we

152 Isaiah 40:31.

shall reap if we do not lose heart. Therefore, as we have opportunity, let us do good to all, especially to those who are of the household of faith."[153]

153 Galatians 6:9–10.

7

Dealing Gracefully with Conflicts in Service

The Sunday School coordinator communicates with so many people. He communicates with the priests of the church, the bishop, the servants, the students, the students' families, and maybe the families of the servants and pre-servants, as well as other churches around them. We are not going to speak about proper communication here, but we will speak mainly about the challenges of communication within the service.

Sometimes, when we communicate in service, we face challenges, and we will take these challenges from Scripture. We see that many challenges and conflicts happened among the apostles, the leaders of the Church. And let us see how they handled these challenges. As St. Paul said, "For whatever things were written before were written for our learning."[154] When we see that our fathers, the apostles, had conflicts with each other, it gives us some peace in our hearts. Not to encourage conflicts among us, but rather, if we find ourselves in a conflict, we should not fall into despair, saying that the service is bad, and there is no hope in rectifying the service in this church, and so on.

1. Power Struggle

The first challenge is the power struggle. There can be a power struggle between two priests, between the priest and the Sunday school coordinator, or between the priest and the deacon coordinator. This is especially likely to happen when there is a Sunday school coordinator who has served for a long time in a church, and a new priest is ordained. Many times, Satan will attack the new priest with insecurity. Who will have the final word in the church? Is it the Sunday school coordinator or me?

This can also happen between the servants and the Sunday school coordinator. For example, some servants have been serving for a long time in the church, and then the priest sees that someone who recently moved to the church is equipped to be a Sunday school coordinator. When he appoints him to be a Sunday school coordinator, all the older servants who have been serving for many years start to wonder who this new person is whom the priest appointed? They say, "Did he find no one among us who is suitable for this service, that he should decide to appoint this person from outside?"

154 Romans 15:4.

There are many examples of power struggles in service, and if we do not handle the power struggles in the right way, they result in division. People will support this person or that person. Once we have division, as the Lord said, "If a house is divided against itself, that house cannot stand."[155] That is why we need to avoid power struggles. A true father or a true Sunday school coordinator is the one who works for the unity of the church more than demanding that his word be done or that he may have the final word.

In the Scripture, we have many examples of power struggles. One famous example can be found in the Gospel of St. Matthew:

> Then the mother of Zebedee's sons came to Him with her sons, kneeling down and asking something from Him. And He said to her, "What do you wish?" She said to Him, "Grant that these two sons of mine may sit, one on Your right hand and the other on the left, in Your kingdom." But Jesus answered and said, "You do not know what you ask. Are you able to drink the cup that I am about to drink, and be baptized with the baptism that I am baptized with?" They said to Him, "We are able." So He said to them, "You will indeed drink My cup, and be baptized with the baptism that I am baptized with; but to sit on My right hand and on My left is not Mine to give, but it is for those for whom it is prepared

155 Mark 3:25.

> by My Father." And when the ten heard it, they were greatly displeased with the two brothers.[156]

Tension began to arise among the disciples. How did the Lord handle it? He told them:

> You know that the rulers of the Gentiles lord it over them, and those who are great exercise authority over them. Yet it shall not be so among you; but whoever desires to become great among you, let him be your servant. And whoever desires to be first among you, let him be your slave— just as the Son of Man did not come to be served, but to serve, and to give His life a ransom for many.[157]

When you get into a power struggle, ask yourself, "Why am I insisting on my opinion? Is it for the betterment of the service? Or because of my ego and my pride? Am I upset because the priest is not giving me the proper prestige among the servants? Is it because of my ego or because of the service?"

A very interesting thing is that power struggles can happen even after Communion, that is, after we attend the Divine Liturgy and take Communion. In the Gospel of St. Luke, after the Lord gave them His Body and Blood, the Scripture says, "Now there was also a dispute among them, as to which of them should be considered

---

156 Matthew 20:20–24.

157 Matthew 20:25–28.

the greatest."[158] The mother of St. John and St. James told Him, let one of them sit on Your right hand and the other on Your left. When they saw the royal entry into Jerusalem, they thought Jesus would be an earthly king. So, another dispute happened among them as to which of them should be considered the greatest. And again, the Lord said the same answer, "The kings of the Gentiles exercise lordship over them, and those who exercise authority over them are called 'benefactors.' But not so among you; on the contrary, he who is greatest among you, let him be as the younger, and he who governs as he who serves."[159]

If the tension happens once, twice, or three times, do not give up. Here, the apostles, the leaders of Christianity in the whole world, had a dispute even after they took Communion. Therefore, be patient, and know that through humility, taking the last seat, and putting the betterment of the service as number one—not you—the problem of power struggle will be resolved.

2. Conflict about the Evaluation of Servants

The second conflict is regarding the evaluation of servants. For example, the priest may consider that a person is fitting to serve, but you, as a Sunday school coordinator, have your own concerns. Then a conflict between you and the priest happens about this. So, how can you resolve this issue?

158 Luke 22:24.

159 Luke 22:25–26.

We have the story of Barnabas and Paul. When they disputed and had a conflict over the evaluation of St. Mark. St. Paul considered that St. Mark was not a good servant because, in the first missionary trip, he left them in Pamphylia and did not continue the first missionary trip. And so he refused to take him on the second missionary trip. Barnabas had a different opinion about St. Mark, and he said that, although St. Mark was young, he was now trained, so let us give him a second chance, and maybe he has an excuse for why he had left them in Pamphylia. Barnabas insisted that St. Mark is a good person and that he should receive another chance. Maybe there was a bias toward Mark since Barnabas was his uncle. Unfortunately, they were not able to solve this conflict, and as we read in the Book of Acts, "Then the contention became so sharp that they parted from one another. And so Barnabas took Mark and sailed to Cyprus; but Paul chose Silas and departed, being commended by the brethren to the grace of God."[160]

Here, there is a mutual understanding about the idea of giving a second chance and a third chance, which is very important. I am sure all of us, in certain situations, were granted a second or third chance. I want you to imagine similar situations in your own life, for example, when you made a mistake in your job. Or when you were a student, you made a mistake, and you asked for a second chance, and it was granted to you. What if you were not granted a second chance? Maybe you would not have a job now, or maybe you would not have graduated

160 Acts 15:39–40.

from school, and so on. The idea of giving a second and third chances to students and trying to make programs to help them improve is very important.

For example, if the priest said that this person was not qualified, the answer is not to just dismiss them and make them leave the service. In companies, when they see a person is not doing well in his evaluation, they bring a mentor to train this person and try to work with them to improve. And indeed, many people benefit from this second chance. And the company benefits also because they have not lost this employee. We need to have this mindset in the church, and we need to consider giving a second, a third, and a fourth chance. But do not just tell the person that you are giving them another chance, and that is it. No, make a program, choose a mentor to help them, and try to train them.

St. Mark, about whom St. Paul said that he could not go with him on the second trip, came to Egypt and became our father, because he was given another chance, and he brought Christianity to the land of Egypt. St. Paul himself changed his opinion about St. Mark. In his second epistle to St. Timothy, St. Paul said, "Get Mark and bring him with you, for he is useful to me for ministry."[161] He changed his opinion about St. Mark. So, try to give a second and a third chance with an empowering program.

Also in this story, we can see the stubbornness and unwillingness to yield—may St. Paul and Barnabas forgive me for utilizing this story. St. Paul insisted on his opinion,

161 2 Timothy 4:11.

and Barnabas did likewise, and they were not able to come to a compromise. They were not able to come to the middle ground. When St. James spoke about heavenly wisdom, he said, "But the wisdom that is from above is first pure, then peaceable, gentle, willing to yield, full of mercy and good fruits."[162] Yes, when it comes to doctrine, do not yield. But many administrative issues sometimes carry tension because we are very opinionated. We are not willing to yield. And this can cause conflict. Some people are described as easygoing, and everyone loves to deal with them. They are flexible, willing to yield, not stubborn, not very opinionated. I think being stubborn or opinionated can be a very big challenge in the service. Therefore, let us acquire this heavenly wisdom that makes us willing to yield when it is needed.

3. Identifying the Root of the Problem

Another problem we can see in the same conflict between Paul and Barnabas is that, in St. Paul's eyes, he saw that Mark was not committed. And I believe that the issues of commitment and dedication come up frequently in our servants' meetings. And here, we need to study the situation. If I have servants who are not committed, again, the solution is not to dismiss them or ask them to leave the service, but we need to identify the reasons why they are not committed. And maybe, what we demand from them is not practical, so we need to find a good balance.

162 James 3:17.

Let us take two stories. In the first one, Pope Shenouda told us that when he was a Sunday school servant, he gave a beautiful lesson about how to keep the day of the Lord, Sunday, holy. And then after he gave this beautiful lesson, he asked the class, "Who is coming this Sunday to the Liturgy?" Nobody raised their hand, so he was greatly disappointed, because he had just spoken to them for about forty minutes about how the day of the Lord should be kept holy. So he started asking them, why? One student said that he had to work on Sunday to provide for his family because they were poor. Another one said that his mother was sick and had to be with her; he could not leave her. Pope Shenouda said that he learned a lesson that day. Not only to prepare a lesson that is powerful, but also practical. You need to understand their real lives and address their needs, so when you give a lesson, you will have a solution for their challenges in life. We need to listen to them and see what their challenges are. Otherwise, our lectures will have nothing to do with their real lives.

This second story happened to me in the past. There was a convention, and I was going with other bishops. I was given the topic of homosexuality. I prepared this matter with references and statistics to make sure that I send a clear message that homosexuality is a sin, and it cannot be accepted. After I finished the lecture, I was happy with myself; I thought it was a very good talk. Someone sent me a question saying, "Your Eminence, I heard so many people speak about homosexuality, saying it is a sin. I know it is a sin, but I am struggling with it. I had hoped that, in your lecture, you would have addressed how one may overcome the sin of homosexuality." This person is right. Most of the time, when we give a lecture on homosexuality, we try to convince people that homosexuality is a sin. But very rarely do we speak about what you should do if you are struggling with homosexuality.

What I am trying to say is that St. Mark was not committed or dedicated. He left them in Pamphylia. Of course, we do not know what the reasons were, but we have to ask ourselves, do we understand our children's real lives, and also the servants we coordinate, before making rules? Before we tell them that they are dismissed from the service because they did not attend the servants' meeting for three consecutive times, and that they can no longer serve, did we understand their real lives or not? This is again a very important element in communication. You need to understand their real lives and the real challenges for each servant. And you cannot do this unless you go and visit them, spend time with them, and ask them about what they are going through, so that you may understand the challenges they are experiencing.

4. Conflict about Doctrine

Another contention happened among the Apostles, but this was regarding the doctrine and dogma. You can see how St. Paul, when it came to doctrine and dogma, did not yield. There was a dispute about how to accept the Gentiles, and this dispute was resolved in the Council of

Jerusalem.[163] St. Paul discovered that when St. Peter went to Antioch in Syria, he sat and ate with the Gentiles, but when some Jews came from Jerusalem to Antioch, he started not to eat with the Gentiles and separated himself from them. Many Jews, when they saw St. Peter doing this, started to do it as well. Even Barnabas did this. As we read in the epistle to the Galatians:

> Now when Peter had come to Antioch, I withstood him to his face, because he was to be blamed; for before certain men came from James, he would eat with the Gentiles; but when they came, he withdrew and separated himself, fearing those who were of the circumcision. And the rest of the Jews also played the hypocrite with him, so that even Barnabas was carried away with their hypocrisy. But when I saw that they were not straightforward about the truth of the gospel, I said to Peter before them all, "If you, being a Jew, live in the manner of Gentiles and not as the Jews, why do you compel Gentiles to live as Jews?[164]

St. Peter was concerned that they would say he was not keeping the Jewish law. So he was not a good example or a role model. He led the Jews to be hypocritical. Here, we can see how St. Paul became very sharp. When there is a dispute about the doctrine or dogma of the Church, we

163 See Acts 15.

164 Galatians 2:11–14.

need to speak the truth but in love. As St. Paul said in his epistle to the Ephesians, "Speaking the truth in love,"[165] because perhaps some people are speaking out of ignorance, and when you teach them, they will be corrected.

When I came to America, I did not know the correct term for the changing of the bread and wine into the Body and the Blood. So I looked the term up in the dictionary and found it to be "transubstantiation." I started to use this term, and I used it out of ignorance. But later on, when I used it, I believe, before Bishop Serapion, he told me that this is a Roman Catholic term, and we do not use it. He explained to me that in our Church, we look at it as a mystery, which is why we do not describe the process of how the bread and wine change into the Body and the Blood. So we use the word "change." I was using a theologically wrong term. I used it out of ignorance, and when somebody told me, I corrected it.

Sometimes, people explain something theologically wrong out of ignorance. Just take the time to explain to them, and they will be convinced and will correct what they said. Do not just become heated and take severe action against this person. At the end, if you find the person is very stubborn and opinionated, and he does not want to accept the true theology, you can discuss it with the priest or bishop, to see what would be the best decision to make. But the point is that, sometimes there is a conflict between the servant and the Sunday school coordinator because of theology, but we need to be alert

165 Ephesians 4:15.

and consider that this dispute can be out of ignorance, and it may present an opportunity to teach them.

5. Different Groups

Conflict may also take place in the service when you have different groups. And this happened in Corinth, where St. Paul found that there were different parties there. People said that they were the children of Paul, others, of Apollos, of Peter, and of Christ. So even Paul was not biased toward those who said that they were children of Paul. He kept his neutrality and told them, "Is Christ divided? Was Paul crucified for you? Or were you baptized in the name of Paul?"[166]

Sometimes having a support group or fans on social media makes us happy. We are the children of so-and-so; we are the fans of so-and-so. All of us should disappear so that Christ may appear and be the center of our service. But unfortunately, sometimes in churches, we may find two schools in the church: the school of this priest or that priest. And instead of complementing one another, they clash with one another. The two schools should not clash with one another but should complement one another. There are definitely different schools in service, but this does not mean that your school is the right school. Do not clash with other people who come from different schools of service. The challenge here is, instead of clashing with one another, to learn how you can complement one another when you come from different schools.

166 1 Corinthians 1:13.

6. Gifts

Another challenge is the challenge between gifts. One of the scenarios is the choir: who will perform in the choir? And we can see this challenge in the first epistle to the Corinthians when some people had the gift of prophecy, and others had the gift of speaking in tongues.[167] They were competing and conflicting with one another wrongfully. St. Paul resolved this issue by telling the people to consider whether this gift was for the edification of the Church or for the edification of the person. If this gift is for the edification of the person or for their own ego, it should not take priority. My own ego should not be considered at all. He explained that if I have the gift of speaking in tongues, yes, I will be edified, but if I speak in tongues, all of you may not understand. But if I prophecy, all of you will learn. That is why he said that he who prophecies is better than he who speaks in tongues, meaning that the gift that benefits the whole church is better than the gift that benefits a few people or one person.

We need to think about this when there is competition between different gifts. How do we organize them in the right priority? What gift is for the benefit of the Church, and what gift is for the benefit of the person or a few people? Again, we should not compete or struggle with one another because of our gifts that are from God. Gifts are tools to edify the Church of God. The best description of gifts is in the epistle to the

167 See 1 Corinthians 14.

Ephesians, "And He Himself gave some to be apostles, some prophets, some evangelists, and some pastors and teachers, for the equipping of the saints for the work of ministry, for the edifying of the body of Christ."[168] And what is the ultimate goal? Edifying the body of Christ. Christ here is the contractor, and we are the workers. The gifts are the equipment that He gave me in order to build this church, the body of Christ.

Can you imagine if a contractor sent some workers and gave them the tools and the equipment they need, and instead of building the structure he wants them to build, they start to fight with each other about the equipment, saying, "My tool is better than your tool!" This building will never be built. Sometimes this happens, and we need to be aware of the goal to edify the body of Christ.

Principles to be Learned from These Conflicts

I would like to put some principles that I extracted from the aforementioned challenges.

Love and Humility. Any communication between us, whether bishop and clergy, clergy and Sunday school coordinator, servants among themselves, if we do not have love and humility, it will not be profitable.

The Benefit of the Service is the Priority. Seeking my own benefit is based on ego, self-centeredness, and selfishness. If what is suitable for all the Sunday school

168 Ephesians 4:11–12.

servants is to have the servants meeting on Sunday, but it is not convenient for me, I can fight and complain to change it, but that is not right, because I am putting my own benefit above the benefit of the service. As Sunday school servants, we need to know how to put the general benefit of the ministry above our own benefit.

Second Chances. Give people second and third chances. All of us were granted a second chance more than once, and because of the second chance, we are where we are right now.

Willingness to Yield. We need to talk to each other to try to come to a happy medium. Try to compromise until we reach a solution that makes everybody happy. As I told you, heavenly wisdom is willing to yield.

Seek Counsel. When it comes to a dispute about theology, doctrine, or dogma in the Church, even St. Paul did not solve it by his own opinion. Maybe his own opinion would have been wrong. That is why he went to the council. So, before you say, "He is wrong, and I am right," maybe you are wrong, and he is right. This is the idea of a council. Go to the priest or bishop. Involve more than one person from the clergy to determine what is right and what is wrong. As we have said, some people make theological mistakes out of ignorance. So sometimes we just need to give them an opportunity.

Develop Servant Training and Improvement Programs. If a servant is not dedicated or you see any weaknesses in their service, try to train them. Try to find a mentor for them or mentor them until they improve.

Seek a Neutral Peacemaker. If there is a conflict between you and one of the servants, or you and the priest, try to find a third person, a peacemaker who is spiritual, who is seeking to make peace and is neutral, not taking any sides. This can be another priest or the bishop who will try to solve the dispute. Do not let the tension turn into a cold war and passive-aggressiveness; otherwise, you will hold grudges in your heart, and these will continue to grow.

One time, about four years ago, I went to Metropolitan Bakhomious and asked him for advice in the ministry. He told me that if there is any issue, tension, or problem, try to solve it on the same day because if you wait, it will escalate. And when it escalates, it will go out of proportion, and solving it will be very difficult. So if there is any conflict, as the Lord told us in the Gospel of St. Matthew, talk to the person. If it is solved, good. If it is not solved, go get two or three people. Get the bishop and another priest, your father of confession, but do not let the contention continue and turn into a cold war, and you start holding grudges against one another. This is not healthy for you, for the other person, or for the service in the Church.

8

Challenges in the Service in the 21st Century

His Holiness Pope Shenouda III—of blessed memory—said that there are no challenges from the outside as long as the Church is strong on the inside. The real challenge comes if the Church loses her spirituality. And this is true. If the Church starts to lose her spirituality, then all these external challenges will influence the Church negatively. But if the Church is strong from within, then all these external challenges cannot affect the Church.

In the era of martyrdom, we see how martyrdom did not divide the Church. Rather, it made the Church stronger. But when divisions happened within the Church—not from outside but from inside, like Nestorianism and Arianism—this is what divided the Church. That is why we will look at the world around us, and how the challenges we face every day may influence the spirituality of the Church. It is a fact that our lives right now are more complex, more stressful, and more demanding. If we compare our lives right now to life twenty-five years ago, they are totally different.

This age is called the information and knowledge worker age. It demands and puts stress on the people, their time, and their effort. That is why we face challenges in our lives, in our families, in our services, and in our churches. And as I said, these challenges did not exist just twenty-five years ago. We will speak about four challenges that are very common in our time, and how they may affect the spirituality of our churches.

1. Living a Dual Life

Nowadays, sin has become more available and more desirable. This is because of contemporary ideologies and philosophies that desensitize us to sin. They do not use the word "sin" anymore. For example, sexual immorality is known as premarital sex. They do not call it immorality or fornication. And they say, "Believe in whatever you want to believe in, and if this makes you feel good, that's okay; there is nothing wrong with it." That is why we see some churches accepting homosexuality as a lifestyle. Also, communication and technology have made sin more available. Now, on the internet, on the computer, and even on your cell phone, you can browse any websites, and for those who are looking for sin and pornography, it is available at the touch of your finger. Twenty-five years ago, this was not the case.

It is also very clear that the media advertises and defends sin. We see many movies defending witchcraft, especially in October. Some media, movies, and music advertise sin and brainwash the minds of our children, desensitizing us to the concept of sin. They even desensitize us to the concept of the authority of God. For example, we use the words tolerance and acceptance, saying we need to tolerate all religions and just have a faith community, regardless of what faith it is. I remember a youth meeting that was attended by about 200 people. When we asked them, "Do you believe that Jesus Christ is the only way to heaven?" 38% of our Coptic youth answered yes. This was very disappointing because our children are exposed to these philosophies outside of the Church, and the media is brainwashing them.

Because of the abundance of sin, with sin becoming more available, we now see many people suffering from fear, shame, and guilt. These are the three consequences of sin: fear, shame, and guilt. And these are the three things that attacked Adam and Eve immediately after they broke the commandment of God. They became afraid, which is why they hid themselves, and Adam said to the Lord, "I heard Your voice in the garden, and I was afraid."[169] They became ashamed. Before falling into sin, the Bible tells us that both of them were naked and unashamed, but after sinning, they became ashamed of themselves. They also experienced guilt because they broke the commandment of God.

169 Genesis 3:10.

That is why we see more people seeking psychological help now. Instead of repenting and returning to God, they try to be on antidepressants and anti-anxiety medications, but maybe this is just a result of living a sinful life. Because of this, the love of God starts to grow cold in the hearts of many people. We find many people coming to church, but their hearts are not as fervent as before. Their zeal is not there. The spirituality and the commitment are not there. The Lord Jesus Christ spoke about our time when he said, "Then many false prophets will rise up and deceive many."[170] I think all of these new philosophies and new ideologies are the false prophets that the Lord spoke about, and that is why they deceive many and have started to desensitize many Christians to sin. What will happen as a result of this? The Lord said, "And because lawlessness will abound, the love of many will grow cold."[171]

That is why, unfortunately, now, the church may be full of unrepentant servants and believers with cold love for God or no love at all. That is why I think we need to repent and return to God with all our hearts. As the Lord said to the angel of one of the seven churches, "You have left your first love. Remember therefore from where you have fallen; repent and do the first works."[172] I think the Church in general, both servants and believers, needs to return wholeheartedly to the Lord, to remember our first love and our first zeal, and to separate ourselves from the

170 Matthew 24:11.

171 Matthew 24:12.

172 Revelation 2:4–5.

sin that is growing in the world. The Greek word *ekklesia* (church) means "called out," called out of the world. So we are called out to be separate from the world; yes, to be in the world but not to be of the world.

In the Book of Jeremiah, the Scripture tells us about how God feels when the church is full of unrepentant servants and believers. God becomes very displeased with this attitude if our love toward Him becomes cold. He said to Jeremiah:

> "Stand in the gate of the LORD's house, and proclaim there this word, and say, 'Hear the word of the LORD, all you of Judah who enter in at these gates to worship the LORD!'" Thus says the LORD of hosts, the God of Israel: "Amend your ways and your doings, and I will cause you to dwell in this place. Do not trust in these lying words, saying, 'The temple of the LORD, the temple of the LORD, the temple of the LORD are these.' For if you thoroughly amend your ways and your doings, if you thoroughly execute judgment between a man and his neighbor, if you do not oppress the stranger, the fatherless, and the widow, and do not shed innocent blood in this place, or walk after other gods to your hurt, then I will cause you to dwell in this place, in the land that I gave to your fathers forever and ever. Behold, you trust in lying words that cannot profit."[173]

173 Jeremiah 7:2–8.

The Lord is directing His words to the people coming to church to worship Him. He is asking them to amend their ways, that is, to repent, and He will make them dwell in this place. He says, "Do not trust in these lying words"; that is, do not just deceive yourself by saying that you are a servant, that you come to church, that you fast the fasts of the Church, without real change and transformation, without returning wholeheartedly to God. You will be the ones who are hurt if you follow other gods and philosophies. And then He challenges them, asking:

> "Will you steal, murder, commit adultery, swear falsely, burn incense to Baal, and walk after other gods whom you do not know, and then come and stand before Me in this house which is called by My name, and say, 'We are delivered to do all these abominations'? Has this house, which is called by My name, become a den of thieves in your eyes? Behold, I, even I, have seen it," says the LORD.[174]

This is the duality of our life, living for the world and also trying to live for God. Unfortunately, for example, some deacons spend Saturday night in an ungodly way, and the next day, they come to church and serve. This duality will not help the church to be strong. God will forsake us because of this duality, as we cannot distinguish light from darkness. Instead of rebuking the works of

---

174 Jeremiah 7:9–11.

darkness, we try to reconcile darkness with light; this is impossible. It is very sad to know that many servants behave in a very ungodly way during wedding receptions and other celebrations. That is exactly what the Lord was speaking to Jeremiah about. This is the abundance of sin that we are addressing.

How are you a servant of the Lord, dedicated and consecrated to His service, and look, now you participate in these works of darkness? Do you believe that, by doing this, you will have a strong Church that can withstand all these challenges from outside? No. That is why the Lord said, "Has this house, which is called by My name, become a den of thieves in your eyes? Behold, I, even I, have seen it."[175] When we live a dual life, living for the world, and also coming to serve in the Church, it is as though we were making this house, which is the Church of God, a den of thieves, as our Lord Jesus Christ said.

Then God said to Jeremiah the prophet:

> "But go now to My place which was in Shiloh, where I set My name at the first, and see what I did to it because of the wickedness of My people Israel. And now, because you have done all these works," says the Lord, "and I spoke to you, rising up early and speaking, but you did not hear, and I called you, but you did not answer, therefore I will do to the house which is called by My name,

---

175 Jeremiah 7:11.

> in which you trust, and to this place which I gave to you and your fathers, as I have done to Shiloh. And I will cast you out of My sight, as I have cast out all your brethren—the whole posterity of Ephraim. Therefore do not pray for this people, nor lift up a cry or prayer for them, nor make intercession to Me; for I will not hear you."[176]

The house in Shiloh became a ruin because of the abominations of Israel. And in the same way, when we live a dual life, the Church of God will become weaker and weaker. We will not be strong enough to withstand the challenges in the world around us. The Lord then says to them that He was speaking and sending His messages to them, but they did not answer Him. As a consequence, He said that He would do to this house as He did to Shiloh and would forsake them as He forsook their brethren; that is, if the people live a dual life. That is why I see this as the first important challenge: living in duality, not separating between sin and righteousness, and trying to combine or reconcile both in our lives. This is the first challenge that the Church is facing, and we need to repent and return to God wholeheartedly.

2. Distractedness and Busyness

Another challenge that affects our service is distractions and our very busy lives. Nowadays, for example, we call our era the cell phone era or the cell phone society. Life in

---

176 Jeremiah 7:12–16.

this age has become very complex, demanding, stressful, and absolutely exhausting. Now, the world is telling us to be more, do more, and achieve greater efficiency. Technology is putting even more pressure on us. That is why, now, many people advertise multitasking, trying to do many things at the same time. Multitasking adds a great deal of pressure and stress on people's lives, which is why we call it "the thick of thin things." You do many activities, but do not do them in the right way or deep enough. That is why many thin things we are doing have become the thick of thin things.

And what will come next in our priorities? Our family, our spirituality, our service, and our integrity. All these things we compromise. Now, the computer is taking time from the family. Each person in the family is spending time on their laptop, and the family unity is threatened by these technologies. Our society advertises going early, staying later, being more efficient, and living with "just sacrifice for now." But you cannot guarantee the future, and this makes us start to lose balance in our lives. That is why many of us also lose our peace of mind. People become very stressed out and anxious because peace of mind and balance can only be found in the person who develops a clear sense of their priorities and who lives with focus and integrity toward these priorities.

When we speak about priorities, we usually classify the priorities into four levels based on whether they are urgent or important. Some tasks are both urgent and important; some tasks are urgent but not important.

Some tasks are important but not urgent. And finally, some are neither urgent nor important. Regarding the first and last priority, there is no disagreement. The priority will go to what is important and urgent. And the last priority will go to what is neither important nor urgent. But the confusion arises regarding which should be the second priority: important but not urgent, or urgent but not important? Many of us do not know how to make the right decision here. Which should come first? Many people may think that, because it is urgent, what is urgent but not important should come before what is important but not urgent. But if you think about it, if it is not important, then this sense of urgency is a false sense of urgency. And many of us operate with this mentality.

An example of what is important but not urgent is spending time with the Holy Scripture. It is very important, but we do not feel it is urgent, so we postpone it. When my cell phone rings, I feel it is urgent, but maybe this call is not as important as the Scripture. So, many times I interrupt my Bible study to answer a phone call. I interrupt my study of the Scripture to waste my time watching the news or TV shows, because I feel an urgency to keep up with the news of the world and to be up to date with all these things. By doing this, I postpone and delay what is important, like my time of prayer, visitation, or preparing my Sunday school lesson. Maybe on Sunday mornings, I open the internet to prepare my Sunday school lesson and just go with what I read in the morning because I did not set my priorities right due to all these distractions. But we need to give higher priority to what is important but does not seem urgent. After this comes what we call urgent but is not important.

The Lord warned us of the busyness of our lives. In the story of Martha and Mary, God blamed Martha, as St. John Chrysostom said, not because she was serving, but because she was busy at the wrong time. She was busy at the time when she should have been sitting at the feet of the Lord, learning from Him. During the Divine Liturgy, if we become busy with other distractions like preparing food or any other activities, we are doing exactly what Martha was doing. We are busy and distracted at the wrong time. There is a time to worship with Mary, and there is a time to serve with Martha.

In the parable of the great supper,[177] the king made a banquet for his son, but the people excused themselves. This is not because they were committing sins, like the first challenge we discussed—the abundance of sin—but because one of them bought a field, the second was married, and the third bought oxen. They just wanted to attend to their work and responsibilities. The king became very angry because they despised his invitation. It is exactly like when we despise the invitation of God to come to the Liturgy, to come to this banquet to celebrate the Eucharist—His Body and His Blood. We are busy with many activities. And God punished them, although it was not mentioned that they had committed any sin. Their sin was being busy during the time of the banquet,

177 See Luke 14:16–24.

being busy during the time of worship, being busy during the time of the Divine Liturgy.

I hear that many servants do not come early enough to the Divine Liturgy. They come late, and then they go to their Sunday school service. How can we do this? Without getting strength from the Divine Liturgy and from Communion with our Lord Jesus Christ, how can I dare to go and teach in the name of the Lord while I am not in communion with Him?

Again, the Lord said in the Gospel of St. Luke about the end of days, "And as it was in the days of Noah, so it will be also in the days of the Son of Man: They ate, they drank, they married wives, they were given in marriage, until the day that Noah entered the ark, and the flood came and destroyed them all."[178] All of these are normal activities; there is nothing wrong with them, but these activities distracted them from serving and worshipping the Lord. And then the Lord continued, saying:

> Likewise as it was also in the days of Lot: They ate, they drank, they bought, they sold, they planted, they built; but on the day that Lot went out of Sodom it rained fire and brimstone from heaven and destroyed them all. Even so will it be in the day when the Son of Man is revealed.[179]

So what is their sin? In the days of Noah and Lot, they were distracted. They were very busy. That is why St.

178 Luke 17:26–27.

179 Luke 17:28–30.

Paul said that we should not live two lives: "Therefore, whether you eat or drink, or whatever you do, do all to the glory of God."[180] We should not let the distractions and the busyness of our lives distract us from serving the Lord.

In the parable of the sower, the Lord said some seeds fell among thorns. What are the thorns? The Lord said the thorns are three things: first, the cares of the world, the many responsibilities, the thick of the thin things; second, the richness, the life of money, wanting to make more money; third, the pleasure of life, just wanting to enjoy yourself and have fun. These three things choke a person. The Lord said, "When they have heard, go out and are choked with cares, riches, and pleasures of life."[181] Not only is the seed choked, which is the word of God, but the person himself will also be choked by these distractions. That is why they bring no fruit to maturity. That is why our lives do not bear the fruit of the Holy Spirit, having no peace or joy. That is why our love is growing cold. As we read in the Gospel of St. Matthew, "Now he who received seed among the thorns is he who hears the word, and the cares of this world and the deceitfulness of riches choke the word, and he becomes unfruitful."[182] That is the reason why we do not have fruit in our lives or in our service.

But why are many people distracted? Why do we yield to this pressure of the world? There are many reasons why

180 1 Corinthians 10:31.

181 Luke 8:14.

182 Matthew 13:22.

we are too busy. If we understand these reasons that make all of us yield to this busyness and distraction, then we may be able to deal with them.

Fear and Insecurity

Many develop a fear of the future. They feel vulnerable in the workplace; they are afraid of losing their jobs, and if they lose their jobs, they may not be able to provide for their families. That is why they want to do more and more for their jobs in order to secure their life, future, and career. Yes, we need to be faithful in our work, but we need to keep the balance, living a balanced life. There is a big difference between being faithful in your work and putting your trust in God. Do not put your trust in anything except God. As St. Paul said, "[God] who delivered us from so great a death, and does deliver us; in whom we trust that He will still deliver us."[183] He said it in the past, present, and future tenses. Be faithful and wise, but do not overburden yourself to the extent that you compromise your service, your relationship with God, your spirituality, your family, and your health. Otherwise, you will be stressed out, and then your performance will be bad. And they will not like you in your work because your performance is bad due to your stress. But if you keep a balanced life, then you will overcome this insecurity.

---

183 2 Corinthians 1:10.

"I Want it Now" Mentality

This society encourages us to get everything now. I want money, and I want it now. I want a nice big house, and I want it now. A nice car, big entertainment center—we say, "I want it all, and I deserve it all." The banks will actually help you. They will tell you to get it now and pay later. Gradually, we fall into this trap, using our credit cards. Eventually, we will find ourselves burdened by major loans and having to pay them every month. I have to pay for the mortgage, for my car, and for this and that. That is why, because I want to get it now, I have to work more and keep myself busy, and so I become distracted, stressed out, and burned out.

Sometimes the demand to pay these loans is very exhausting to the person. That is why even when we are working very hard, it might not be enough to pay all the loans that we have burdened ourselves with. So we need to get rid of this "I want it now" mentality. Let us grow little by little. Let us be content with what we have. As St. Paul said, "I have learned in whatever state I am, to be content: I know how to be abased, and I know how to abound. Everywhere and in all things I have learned both to be full and to be hungry, both to abound and to suffer need. I can do all things through Christ who strengthens me."[184] We need to learn how to be content in order to get rid of this negative attitude of "I want it now."

---

184 Philippians 4:11–13.

Competition

Another reason why we are overworked, stressed out, and distracted is competition. Our society is very competitive. In the workforce, you must not only be educated, but also you should always re-educate and re-invent yourself. Otherwise, they might consider that they do not need you anymore in your work. This competitive society puts a lot of burden on us because we must redevelop our minds and continually re-sharpen our competencies to avoid becoming obsolete.

But here we need to think about what will make us successful in our lives. If we work very hard right now and exhaust our resources, without sustaining this success and growth and development, then maybe we will grow faster, but we will end sooner. That is why the most important question is: Are you making the best investment that will sustain and increase that success for one, five, or ten years? We need to be wise; do not over-exhaust yourself to be more productive right now, and then down the road, you will lose your success. That is why the Church Fathers said that the middle way saved many.

How can we keep a balanced life? The Book of Ecclesiastes says, "To everything there is a season."[185] Even priests, if they do not keep a balanced life, if they overwork and over-exhaust themselves in the service, will gradually become stressed out and burned out, and they will not be able to give peace and joy to others. The

185 Ecclesiastes 3:1.

congregation will see us exhausted and burdened because we do not set the right boundaries.

Let us examine some verses from the Bible to show how our Lord Jesus Christ actually set the right boundaries in service. He had time to rest, time to eat, time to relax, because this helped Him to serve better. I remember that, one time, my spiritual father told me, "If you serve twenty-four hours every day for seven days a week, it will not cover all the demands of the service. That is why you need to take time for yourself, time for your cell, your personal time with Christ to be able to get better and then serve better."

In the Gospel of St. Mark, the Lord Jesus Christ said to His disciples, "Come aside by yourselves to a deserted place and rest a while."[186] St. Mark tells us, "For there were many coming and going, and they did not even have time to eat."[187] Even the Lord Jesus Christ, who told us not to labor for the food which perishes but for the food that does not perish, said to His disciples that they should go to a deserted place and rest a while. They had not eaten, so now it was time to relax and eat.

In another place, the Scripture says:

> Now in the morning, having risen a long while before daylight, He went out and departed to a solitary place; and there He prayed. And Simon and those who were with Him searched for

186 Mark 6:31.

187 Ibid.

> Him. When they found Him, they said to Him, "Everyone is looking for You." But He said to them, "Let us go into the next towns, that I may preach there also, because for this purpose I have come forth."[188]

The Lord did not feel guilty that the people were asking for Him. He told them, "No, I have a responsibility to go to the next town." Many times, when people pressure us to go and visit them, but we may have a full schedule, we feel guilty, or we feel that we are not serving the people faithfully, because we said no to them. But here, the Lord Jesus Christ was keeping His balance. Although many people were asking to see Him, He said, "No, let us go into the next towns."

Again, in the Gospel of St. Mark, we learn that "Jesus could no longer openly enter the city, but was outside in deserted places; and they came to Him from every direction."[189] He felt that being in the city and openly entering the city would distract Him, and He could not do His service properly. That is why He stayed outside in a deserted place, and they came to Him.

All of these examples show us how the Lord Jesus Christ was teaching the disciples not to be distracted, not even by the ministry. Do not let the ministry distract you. In the Gospel of St. Luke, it says, "Now when it was day, He departed and went into a deserted place. And

---

188 Mark 1:35–38.

189 Mark 1:45.

the crowd sought Him and came to Him, and tried to keep Him from leaving them; but He said to them, 'I must preach the kingdom of God to the other cities also, because for this purpose I have been sent.'"[190] See, the Lord was very careful to go to a quiet place to relax, have time with the Father, pray, and have time for meditation and reflection. Although the people wanted to hear the word of God, He did not yield to their pressure. He said to them that He desired to preach in the other cities.

In another place in the Gospel of St. Luke, the Scripture says, "However, the report went around concerning Him all the more; and great multitudes came together to hear, and to be healed by Him of their infirmities. So He Himself often withdrew into the wilderness and prayed."[191] The people came to hear the word of God, but He did not allow this distraction to take away from the time of His prayer. He actually withdrew from them to go to the mountain and pray.

So here, the principle of balancing the need to meet the demands of our day with the need to invest in our ability to produce tomorrow's success is very important. This rule is true for your service, for your health, for your family, for your relationships, in all areas of your life. It is important to keep this balance between meeting the demands of the day and investing in proper relaxation to produce the success of the morrow.

190 Luke 4:42–43.

191 Luke 5:15–16.

3. Suffering and Our Reaction to It

In our lives, it is not a question of whether we will suffer or not. All of us suffer and face hardships. But the way we deal with suffering is very important. In the parable of the sower, if the thorns are the distractions, then the stony land is the hardships and trials. That is why the Lord Jesus Christ said, "But he who received the seed on stony places, this is he who hears the word and immediately receives it with joy; yet he has no root in himself, but endures only for a while. For when tribulation or persecution arises because of the word, immediately he stumbles."[192] So, how can we be fruitful when these hardships come? How can we avoid losing our spirituality even during the time of suffering and hardships?

A common reaction we have when we go through a hardship is to cast the blame on others. This is what happened with Adam and Eve. When God held them accountable, they started to blame one another. We are now addicted to this victim mentality and to blaming others. For example, we may say, "If only my boss weren't such a controlling person." "If only I lived in a better place." "If only I didn't inherit such a temper from my dad." "If only my kids weren't so rebellious." "If only my wife were more understanding." "If only our church were more evangelistic." "If only God did not allow this to happen to me." If only, if only.

We usually cast the blame on even God for what we are going through. Blaming everyone and everything

192 Matthew 13:20–21.

else, including God, for our problems and suffering is the norm for this society. This may give us a sense of transient relief from pain, but this blaming chains and binds us to these very problems, because we are saying there is no solution, no way out of these problems. By doing this, I put all the power to change outside of me. "If these people changed, then my problem would be solved." I put the problem outside of my hands. But if I take responsibility for these hardships and try to figure out what I can do through the grace of God, thinking about what my role should be to solve this problem, I will actually become stronger, and the word of God will not be choked by these rocks and stones in my life, and I will be able to bear fruit in my life.

That is why the Holy Bible teaches us to be humble, accepting and taking responsibility for our circumstances. I must also be courageous enough to do whatever I can and take the initiative in order to work my way through or around this difficulty. Even if nothing can be done, I will endure, and "he who endures to the end will be saved."[193] That is why St. James told us, "My brethren, count it all joy when you fall into various trials, knowing that the testing of your faith produces patience. But let patience have its perfect work, that you may be perfect and complete, lacking nothing."[194] St. James is saying that if you do not endure and are not patient during suffering, you will not be perfect.

193 Matthew 10:22.

194 James 1:2–4.

Our spirituality and service will also struggle. We see how many people, when they go through a difficult time, stop coming to church or stop serving because of their problems. They make a U-turn and completely give their backs to God. As St. James said, "Blessed is the man who endures temptation; for when he has been approved, he will receive the crown of life which the Lord has promised to those who love Him."[195] During hardship, we have to be very cautious in choosing our reaction. Which reaction will we have? Are we going to blame others? Are we going to be resentful? Are we going to accuse God and others, or be humble, accept responsibility, and try to think about what to do through the grace of God? What can I do, which is in my hand, to overcome this situation?

When we blame others and refuse to take responsibility, we will develop hopelessness. As they say, the children of blame are pessimism and hopelessness. Instead of becoming optimistic and hopeful, we become pessimistic. If we believe that we are victims of our circumstances and believe that these things are predetermined, with no way to avoid them, we start to lose hope, lose the drive, lose motivation, and settle into resignation and stagnation. That is why many bright and talented people fall into this trap and become victims of depression and discouragement. This is because they fell into the trap of hopelessness after blaming others and developing a victim mentality. Our society teaches us to lower our expectations in life to the point that we are not

195 James 1:12.

disappointed by anyone or anything. That is how society teaches us to survive during difficult times.

But let us see what the Bible teaches us about surviving during difficult times. When St. Paul suffered from a thorn in the flesh, he prayed that God might heal him, and the Lord told him, "No, I will not heal you." Then St. Paul asked, "If you are not going to heal me, how will I survive this hardship?" The Lord told him, "My grace is sufficient for you, for My strength is made perfect in weakness."[196] St. Paul responded, "Therefore most gladly I will rather boast in my infirmities, that the power of Christ may rest upon me. Therefore I take pleasure in infirmities, in reproaches, in needs, in persecutions, in distresses, for Christ's sake. For when I am weak, then I am strong."[197]

When you go through a difficult time, when you are among the rocks and the stones, do not let these rocks and stones make you hopeless, but rather turn your eyes to Christ, to the heavens, and you will find that God is supporting you. This is exactly what happened to St. Stephen. He was in the pit, and they were stoning him. He did not look at the stones, but switched his focus and looked to heaven. He saw Christ standing in heaven, and he saw the crowns that were prepared for him; that is why he was able to forgive. He was able to pray for those who were killing him because he switched his focus. Many times, we lower our eyes from Christ to look at

196 2 Corinthians 12:9.

197 2 Corinthians 12:9–10.

the stones. Like St. Peter, when he lowered his eyes, he started to drown. When his eyes were fixed on the Lord Jesus Christ, he did not drown. But once he looked at the storm and the wind, he started to drown. So, how do we survive during times of hardship? Just keep your eyes focused and fixed on the Lord Jesus Christ.

I want to emphasize that we should not only do this during the time of suffering, but also during the time of sin. What do I mean by the time of sin? When St. Peter denied the Lord Jesus Christ, we read in the Bible that "the Lord turned and looked at Peter."[198] The question here is: how did Peter know that the Lord Jesus Christ was looking at him? Because his eyes were fixed on our Lord Jesus Christ. So, not only did Jesus look at Peter, but Peter was also looking at our Lord Jesus Christ. When his eyes made contact with the eyes of Christ, he felt his sins. He was denying Jesus, but his eyes were on Christ, and he was able to repent and be healed. As long as my eyes are on heaven, on the Lord Jesus Christ, then I can survive. Even in hardships, in the time of suffering, even when I sin, because His eyes help me to repent. Looking at our Lord Jesus Christ will develop in me "godly sorrow produces repentance leading to salvation, not to be regretted."[199]

4. Superficial Spirituality

The third type of land is the road or the wayside. The seed that fell on the way represents superficiality, that is,

198 Luke 22:61.

199 2 Corinthians 7:10.

when our spirituality is superficial or ritualistic. Being only ritualistic is an external form of religion with no real transformation from within. This is another thing that will kill our spirituality, because the birds will come and eat these seeds. With all these distractions and the abundance of lawlessness, our spirituality is gone, and we descend into ritualistic spirituality. This is the worship that focuses on the rituals while completely neglecting spirituality or the inner transformation. We keep the outside form of religion, but not the real relationship with Christ. That is why we say that rituals without spirituality are idolatry.

For example, a servant may ask their Sunday school students the following questions: Why did you not attend Sunday school last week? Did you attend the Liturgy? Did you take Communion? When was the last time you confessed? Do you read the Bible? All these questions are good, but they all focus on the external form of worship. For example, if they say, "Yes, I read the Bible." Then I am happy as a servant. But did I teach them how to benefit from the Bible? How to turn the words of the Bible into life? They should not merely study the word of God with their mind, but they must keep the words in their heart and allow the word of God to transform them.

When I ask about Communion, it is not just standing in the line and partaking of the Body and Blood of our Lord Jesus Christ. It is being in union with Christ, to be in a relationship. So if I ask them when the last time was that they confessed, and they say, "I have not confessed for a long time," I cannot simply say, "Okay, go tomorrow to confess and take Communion." They may go to the priest with no repentance and just say some sins. After they say some sins, the next day they will stand in line and take Communion, but there is no transformation, no real change.

That is what I am calling ritualistic spirituality, because there is no change on the inside. I am happy because they came, attended the Liturgy, and took Communion, but they are totally disconnected from God. We need to reconnect the people to God. That is why St. Paul said, "Now then, we are ambassadors for Christ, as though God were pleading through us: we implore you on Christ's behalf, be reconciled to God."[200] Being reconciled to Christ is to be reconnected to Christ. Many people keep these rituals but are totally disconnected. The same applies to fasting. Fasting is not only changing the type of food, but it is also to develop self-control and to use this against sin, to be able to say no to sin.

In order to focus on spirituality, it is not enough to ask about these practices. But we need to explain the deeper meaning of these practices. If you hear of a baby who is going to be baptized, consider what Baptism is. Baptism is to die with Christ and rise with Him. This meaning should be clear in the minds of the parents. They are raising this child to be dead to the world and alive to Christ. That is Baptism: to say, "It is no longer I who live, but Christ lives in me."[201]

200 2 Corinthians 5:20.

201 Galatians 2:20.

When the Lord Jesus Christ taught us how to pray, fast, and do charitable deeds, He focused on this. Yes, the rituals and the external practices are very important. I am not belittling them because they are the tools that help me reach this inner relationship with Christ. But if I just focus on these external practices with no real inner relationship with Christ, they are useless. Even when we do visitations, we just want to check it off our list. I visited five people this week—check. It is like I am just fulfilling an obligation. I am too busy, so I just want to finish it. It is an obligation, not quality time. It is not a time that I spend with this person, rejoicing together and enjoying the presence of God among us.

How about our Sunday school lessons? Maybe on Sunday morning, I will go on the internet to check which lesson is scheduled for Sunday school today. I am just doing the practice, but there is no depth to it. It is like the seed on the road, on the surface, with no depth. That is why there is no fruit; it is fruitless. And that is why we see our youth and our children so disconnected from God in their lives. Where is our relationship with God? Where is our relationship with one another? We must understand that these practices are not the goal; they are just the means to our goal, which is God. Rituals without spirituality will lead to a Church full of leaves but no fruit, like the fig tree that was full of leaves but had no fruit. The Lord rebuked the scribes and Pharisees, and cursed the fig tree for this reason. They were tithing mint and cummin and anise, but they were very far from the weightier matters of the law of God.[202] That is why we need to be very careful lest we be making or raising hypocrites, not spiritual persons, lest we be teaching our children hypocrisy, only making sure they maintain the checklist. They know the practices they should do, but without any real transformation in their lives.

Many challenges threaten our spirituality. If the Church loses her spirituality, she will not be strong enough to withstand attacks from outside. Without returning to God, Scripture, and the holy Church Fathers, it is impossible to cope and build a strong spiritual Church.

202 See Matthew 23:23.

9

The Virtue of Endurance in Service

Let us read a passage from the Book of Sirach:

> Son, when you apply yourself to the service of God, stand in justice and in fear, and prepare your soul for temptation. Humble your heart, and persevere. Incline your ear, and accept words of understanding. And you should not hurry away in the time of distress. Endure steadfastly for God. Join yourself to God, and persevere, so that your life may increase in the very end. Accept everything that will happen to you, and persevere in your sorrow, and have patience in your humiliation. For gold and silver are tested in fire, yet truly, acceptable men are tested in the furnace of humiliation. Believe God, and he will

> restore you to health. And straighten your way, and hope in him. Observe his fear, and grow old in it.[1]

This part is very important to us as Sunday school servants. Also in monasticism, when we consecrate a monk or a nun, we read three prophecies, including this one. The focus in this part of the Book of Sirach is the importance of endurance. How can you prepare yourself for the service of God? You need to prepare yourself to endure distress, humiliation, and hardship. This is how we prepare ourselves to serve the Lord. Some people, when they serve God and find that there are challenges, consider leaving or quitting the service, but this should not be the case. The case, as we read in Sirach, should be that we learn how to endure, stay steadfast, and persevere.

All the people of God endured. St. Mary, the Mother of God, endured. She knew that when she became pregnant, she would be accused of adultery, and there would be no justification or defense for her. When she accepted to carry the Son of God in her womb, she also accepted to endure suffering. She did not know what would happen to her, but she trusted that God would defend her. I am sure that all of you know that even St. Joseph doubted her purity.

All the martyrs endured. They endured to the point of shedding their blood. The confessors endured torture. St. Samuel the confessor endured one of his eyes being plucked out because he refused to sign the Tome of Leo,

1 Sirach 2:1–6 CPDV.

and he tore it apart. All the saints endured. We endure hardships in life. So to endure for the sake of God is better than just enduring. Our life here is not easy. We suffer from illnesses, hardships, financial distress, death, and the loss of loved ones.

As Christians, we are persecuted. Oftentimes at work, school, in the family, among our friends, even sometimes in the church, we suffer injustice and unfairness. When we learn how to endure and how to cope, this will be good for our relationship with God and will also help us learn how to endure in the world. Endurance will make us perfect, lacking nothing. St. James said, "My brethren, count it all joy when you fall into various trials."[2] Why? Why should I count it all joy? The explanation of St. James is, "Knowing that the testing of your faith produces patience."[3] Endurance means I will be patient. "But let patience have its perfect work, that you may be perfect and complete, lacking nothing."[4] I must endure to the end, as the Lord said, "He who endures to the end will be saved."[5] When we learn how to endure for the sake of God, we will be perfect and complete, lacking nothing.

Endurance is not a negative or a passive stance. Endurance is a positive stance. There is a difference between saying, "What can I do? I have no choice; I have to put up with this," and saying, "By my own will, I choose to endure." That is why the Lord Jesus Christ told

2 James 1:2.

3 James 1:3.

4 James 1:4.

5 Matthew 10:22.

us that if someone slaps you on your right cheek, turn the other one.[6] Why do I turn the other one? To say that my endurance is not passive, but rather it is active. That is why I am willingly turning the other cheek if you want to slap me again. The Lord told us that if someone compels you to walk one mile, walk with him two.[7] Walking the second mile is saying that I chose to walk with him the first mile, and by my own will, I am choosing to walk with him the second mile, willingly. Similarly, if someone wants to take your garment, give him your cloak also.[8] Again, this means I am leaving my cloak and my garment willingly.

When you do not endure but rather get into fights and power struggles, you lose your peace, thankfulness, and joy. But when you willingly endure, you will be peaceful, you will be joyful, and you will be content.

However, our endurance is not out of weakness, because when it comes to faith, no, I am not going to deny my faith. I will stand firm and say, "No, I do not believe in this. I will not worship idols. I am not going to deny my Christ." Endurance is not weakness or a passive attitude, but it is an active, positive attitude. Like St. Samuel the confessor, when they brought to him the Tome of Leo, he rejected it and tore it, and he would not sign it. He rejected it out of strength, not weakness. What I am trying to say is that endurance is founded on strength and not weakness.

---

6 See Matthew 5:39.

7 See Matthew 5:41.

8 See Matthew 5:40.

We also have our weaknesses. I want others to endure me, put up with my weaknesses, and accept me. Therefore, I should also endure the weaknesses of others. It is unfair to expect that others endure my weaknesses if I do not endure their weaknesses. What is surprising here is that we are called to endure and accept injustice and unfairness. We are called to this. St. Peter said, "Servants, be submissive to your masters with all fear, not only to the good and gentle, but also to the harsh. For this is commendable, if because of conscience toward God one endures grief, suffering wrongfully."[9] You are enduring because this is the teaching of Christianity. You are willing to endure grief and suffer wrongfully. Suffering wrongfully means without having committed any mistake. Then he says, "For what credit is it if, when you are beaten for your faults, you take it patiently? But when you do good and suffer, if you take it patiently, this is commendable before God."[10] If I did something wrong and I am beaten for my faults and I take it patiently, I deserve the punishment. However, when I do good and then suffer, although what I did was right and good, and I endure patiently because of conscience toward God, this is commendable and praiseworthy before God.

St. Peter then says, "For to this you were called, because Christ also suffered for us, leaving us an example, that you should follow His steps."[11] "This" means to endure grief and suffer wrongfully but with patience. We

9 1 Peter 2:18–19.

10 1 Peter 2:20.

11 1 Peter 2:21.

are called to this. As Christians, we are called to endure. What is the example Christ left us, and how should we follow His steps? He explained, "[Jesus], 'who committed no sin, nor was deceit found in His mouth'; who, when He was reviled, did not revile in return; when He suffered, He did not threaten, but committed Himself to Him who judges righteously; who Himself bore our sins in His own body on the tree, that we, having died to sins, might live for righteousness—by whose stripes you were healed."[12] That is the example of our Lord Jesus Christ, and he wants us to follow in His steps.

The same concept is again repeated in the same epistle, where he says,

> Having a good conscience, that when they defame you as evildoers, those who revile your good conduct in Christ may be ashamed. For it is better, if it is the will of God, to suffer for doing good than for doing evil. For Christ also suffered once for sins, the just for the unjust, that He might bring us to God, being put to death in the flesh but made alive by the Spirit.[13]

We are called to endure. If my friend, a family member, or anyone treats me wrongfully, I need to endure and forgive. This is because love "endures all things."[14] Do you know why we lack endurance?

---

12 1 Peter 2:22–24.

13 1 Peter 3:16–18.

14 1 Corinthians 13:7.

Because we do not have this love. The fruit of the Holy Spirit is love, but we do not have it. People fight with each other. People abandon each other. People avoid each other. Why? For lack of love. If we truly love one another, we will endure.

In the passage from the epistle to the Ephesians, which the Church calls us to pray in the first hour of the Agpeya, we read that we need to "walk worthy of the calling with which you were called, with all lowliness and gentleness, with longsuffering, bearing with one another in love, endeavoring to keep the unity of the Spirit in the bond of peace."[15]

There are divisions in the family, divisions in the Church, divisions among friends. Why? Because of the lack of endurance and the lack of love. When we learn how to endure, then peace and unity will be among us. The Church will be in unity. Families will be in unity. Brothers and sisters, husband and wife, parents and children will be in unity.

The most important question is, how do we endure? In service, you will face challenges. You might be falsely accused by your students or by the parents of your students. Or you might suffer some unfairness or injustice from the leaders in the church. But are you willing to endure or not? We will talk about seven points that will help you endure.

15 Ephesians 4:1–3.

1. Love

We need to grow in the virtue of love. If you love someone, you will let go of many things. But if you do not love a person, you will be lying in wait to catch them at something. Love is the key to endurance. When blaming others and saying, for example, "This person is intolerable," the problem is not in the other person; the problem is in you. You do not have enough love to endure and tolerate them. There is a big difference between tolerating a person and tolerating sin. I am speaking about tolerating the person and not the sin.

2. Patience

The second virtue that you need is patience, to endure patiently. As St. James said, if you are patient, you will be perfect, complete, and lacking nothing.[16] We are in a time in which everything is very fast. We connect to the internet quickly, and when we load a page, if it takes more than three seconds, we get frustrated. Similarly, we are not patient with one another, nor do we endure each other. That is why the Bible gave us the story of Job, to learn from him the life of endurance. St. James says, "My brethren, take the prophets, who spoke in the name of the Lord, as an example of suffering and patience. Indeed we count them blessed who endure. You have heard of the perseverance of Job and seen the end intended by the Lord—that the Lord is very compassionate and

---

16 See James 1:4.

merciful."[17] Therefore, if you endure, you will be blessed. If you refuse to endure, then you will not be blessed.

At times in our spiritual life, we do not want to persevere. Sometimes I quit a certain sin for a few days, and as soon as I get the desire to go back to the sin, I relapse. I do not fight the good fight. This is a lack of endurance, a lack of patience. Think about Job; he lost everything. He lost his children, he lost his money, he lost his health. But in all these things, he did not blame God but endured patiently. How was Job able to endure and to be patient?

St. Paul said, "Be transformed by the renewing of your mind."[18] What does that mean? If I change my mindset, if I try to think differently about the situation, then I will be able to accept it and will be able to endure. The renewal of your mind is the key. Sometimes we dwell on a certain idea, but if we look at it from a different perspective, then we will be fine with it and will accept it. For example, let us go back to Job. How was Job able to accept? He said, "Naked I came from my mother's womb, and naked shall I return there. The Lord gave, and the Lord has taken away; blessed be the name of the Lord."[19] This way of thinking gave him acceptance.

This way of thinking made it easy for Job to endure. Even when his wife told him, "Do you still hold fast

17 James 5:10–11.

18 Romans 12:2.

19 Job 1:21.

to your integrity? Curse God and die!"[20] Job answered her and said, "You speak as one of the foolish women speaks. Shall we indeed accept good from God, and shall we not accept adversity?"[21] His wife needed to change her mindset, to renew her mind, to think differently, to accept it. You can think foolishly, or you can think wisely. If you think foolishly, then you will be full of anger and bitterness, and you will refuse to endure. But if you think wisely, then you can endure.

3. Divine Grace

To endure, you need grace from above. You need to ask God to support you and give you this grace. How did the Lord Jesus Christ prepare Himself to endure the suffering of the cross? St. Paul says about Christ, "Who, in the days of His flesh, when He had offered up prayers and supplications, with vehement cries and tears to Him who was able to save Him from death, and was heard because of His godly fear."[22] Even the Lord Jesus Christ, to prepare Himself for the cross, offered prayers, supplications, vehement cries, and tears. The Lord did this in Gethsemane, to the extent that His sweat became like drops of blood.

If you go through adversity or if you believe that you are treated unfairly or unjustly, go into your inner room, get on your knees, offer prayers and supplications

---

20 Job 2:9.

21 Job 2:10.

22 Hebrews 5:7.

with vehement cries and tears to God, who can save you from death. And indeed, Jesus died on the cross but rose on the third day. That is why St. Paul said, "And [He] was heard because of His godly fear." You cannot endure without divine grace, without support from above.

4. Understanding the Weaknesses of Others

You need to understand and empathize with the weaknesses of others. St. Paul says, "We then who are strong ought to bear with the scruples of the weak, and not to please ourselves. Let each of us please his neighbor for his good, leading to edification. For even Christ did not please Himself."[23]

Sometimes we do not endure because we want to please ourselves. Why would a couple fight with each other? Because each one wants their will to be done. Each one wants to please themselves. But St. Paul told us that if you count yourself strong, then you need to bear with the scruples of the weak and not to please yourself. If someone is paralyzed, do you expect him to carry you or help you? The strong should bear with the scruples of the weak. Just as you want others to bear with your scruples, you need to bear with the scruples of others. Understand the weaknesses of others. No one is perfect. Therefore, we need to encourage one another, to forgive one another, and to endure one another to keep the peace, love, and unity among us.

---

23 Romans 15:1–3.

5. Looking to the Reward

Let me tell you a story that will help explain two verses from the Scripture. A father had two sons. One of them was a complainer. He complained constantly, saying, "My brother did this to me. My brother is bothering me." The father wanted to teach his son how to be grateful and to endure, not to be a complainer. So he told him that every time his brother bothered him, he should come and take $200. So now, this son is looking for money. Every time his brother bothers him, he is happy and no longer complains. Instead, he goes to his father to get his $200.

This is exactly what the Lord told us in the sermon on the mount, saying, "Blessed are you when they revile and persecute you, and say all kinds of evil against you falsely for My sake. Rejoice and be exceedingly glad, for great is your reward in heaven."[24] Every time I am persecuted, every time I am slandered, every time I am reviled, God adds to my reward in heaven. If you look to the reward, you can endure.

If you look at the reviling and slandering, however, you will be angry. Look to the reward. In the epistle to the Hebrews, St. Paul says about the Lord Jesus Christ Himself, "Looking unto Jesus, the author and finisher of our faith, who for the joy that was set before Him endured the cross, despising the shame."[25] So how did the Lord endure the cross? He was looking to the joy: the joy of salvation, the joy of the resurrection, the joy of destroying

24 Matthew 5:11–12.

25 Hebrews 12:2.

Hades and bringing all the souls of the righteous to the Paradise of joy, the joy of defeating sin, the joy of defeating the devil, the joy of defeating the pleasures of the world.

When St. Stephen was being stoned, if he had looked at the stones, he may have fallen into self-pity, saying, "I didn't do anything wrong; why are they killing me? Why are they stoning me?" But St. Stephen looked to heaven, and he saw heaven open and the Son of Man standing at the right hand of the Father. When he saw this glory and knew that after a few minutes he would be there, he said to the Lord, "These people are not actually killing me; they are rather giving me this glory. Oh Lord, do not charge them with this sin." There is logic behind his prayer, "Lord, do not charge them with this sin."[26] This is the renewal of his mind. When he looked at it differently, he was able not only to endure but also to pray for them, which means that endurance is not passive but active.

6. Hope

Things will not continue in the same way forever. Adversity will not last forever; neither will financial burdens nor illnesses. Have hope. His Holiness Pope Shenouda used to say three phrases, which helped him to endure and deal with all the challenges that he faced in his ministry. These are three simple sayings that serve as a scripture for endurance. The first one is "God is present." God exists; God is with us. The second one is, "It is bound to come to an end." And the third one is, "All things are for good."

26 Acts 7:60.

The First Phrase. If I know that God is present—God is with me—then who can be against me, as St. Paul said, "If God is for us, who can be against us?"[27] God has control over the authorities, the leaders, and over the whole world. And we remember what happened in September, 1981, how President Sadat had a very bad plan against the Church, His Holiness Pope Shenouda, and many bishops, clergy, and lay people. But all this changed in less than one month because God is with us. And if God is with us, nobody can be against us. Nothing will hurt you except with permission from God.

The Second Phrase. If God allowed it, then we trust that "all things work together for good to those who love God."[28] All things—even martyrdom. Yes, sometimes people might be delivered, as it happened in 1981. But at other times, like the martyrs of Libya or the many martyrs over the centuries, God did not allow them to be delivered, but it was for their good. And we should know that all things work out for good. St. Paul did not say, "most of the time," or "most probably, all things work out for good," but he said, "all things," with no exception.

The Third Phrase. "It is bound to come to an end." This adversity of 1981 ended, and now it is history. People who were in prison were released. Pope Shenouda was released from house arrest, and it ended. Therefore, be patient. Endure. When we were allowed to visit the monastery and meet His Holiness, he was always joking,

---

27 Romans 8:31.

28 Romans 8:28.

happy, and smiling. He did not allow the trial to take his joy away nor his peace because he trusted in God. He trusted that God is in charge. God is in control and can miraculously change everything. Have hope in God.

7. Support System

Our main support system is the intercession of the saints. In the epistle to the Hebrews, St. Paul says, "Therefore we also, since we are surrounded by so great a cloud of witnesses, let us lay aside every weight, and the sin which so easily ensnares us, and let us run with endurance the race that is set before us."[29] This cloud of witnesses is praying for you and supporting you through their prayers before God. That is why when we enter the church, we see the icons of the saints surrounding us from all directions, reminding us that we are not alone. We are surrounded by a cloud of witnesses. They encourage us, pray for us, and support us.

The virtue of endurance is very important to all Christians, and more importantly, to servants. As we read in the second chapter of the Book of Sirach, he repeated several times that you need to endure. You need to bear with one another. You need to persevere. You need to be patient. All this terminology, unfortunately, is not acceptable right now. People now focus on human rights, saying, "That is my right. I have to defend my rights." We need to do what is right and to endure for the sake of God.

29 Hebrews 12:1.

Love, and do what you will: whether you hold your peace, through love hold your peace; whether you cry out, through love cry out; whether you correct, through love correct; whether you spare, through love do spare: let the root of love be within, of this root can nothing spring but what is good.

St. Augustine of Hippo

Homilies on the First Epistle of John,
Homily 7.8

www.ingramcontent.com/pod-product-compliance
Lightning Source LLC
Chambersburg PA
CBHW022000150726
47990CB00002B/538

* 9 7 9 8 8 9 4 8 3 0 5 3 7 *